SELECTED POEMS

SELECTED POEMS

JENNY BORNHOLDT

VICTORIA UNIVERSITY PRESS

TE WHARE WĀNANGA O TE ŪPOKO O TE IKA A MĀUI
VICTORIA
UNIVERSITY OF WELLINGTON

VICTORIA UNIVERSITY PRESS
Victoria University of Wellington
PO Box 600 Wellington
vup.victoria.ac.nz

First published 2016

National Library of New Zealand Cataloguing-in-Publication Data

Bornholdt, Jenny, 1960-
Selected poems / Jenny Bornholdt.
ISBN 978-1-77656-066-0
I. Title.
NZ821.2—dc 23

Published with the assistance of a grant from

creative nz
ARTS COUNCIL OF NEW ZEALAND TOI AOTEAROA

Printed by 1010 Printing International

Contents

I. WEIGHING UP THE HEART

II. THESE DAYS

III. PEARLY EVERLASTING

for Greg

I. WEIGHING UP THE HEART

Scrub cut

I

These hairs like
fern fingers
curl on my arm
dropped there during
the tree felling
the scrub cutting
the letting in of light.

You have trimmed away
the undergrowth
making way

There is now no saying
'That is Manuka.
That is Rimu.
Look, there is a Pohutukawa
that will have red flowers
of this particular shade,
with the needles falling.'

II

This bristly crop
tells of nothing but
beginnings.
Here it is, here I am
grinning out at you from
this big face.

In the garden

In the garden
the bulbs run riot
root systems go
all over the place
we crack open huge dry
clods of earth and uncover
white bulbs of onion flowers
embedded like fossils
their roots like thin streamers
partying down through the soil.
So we have a white flower
propped on the top of a green stem
a plain enough thing
while underneath
the feelers are out
hooking into other systems
forming the network
the flower an undercover agent
posted on the watch
a decoy of simplicity.

A love poem has very long sentences

This is a sort of love poem
it has some long sentences
one in particular is very long.

That is because there can be a lot to say
in a sort of love poem
sorting out the sort of from the is, for instance
trying to get it all down
for example: the silent blue of water
the sound of fallen leaves on a bare throat
the movement of trees
the dissolve of skin on skin
the crack of thin white bones

there is a lot you can say in a
sort of love poem
it probably helps to have some long sentences
and there is nothing to be ashamed of
in having one in particular that is very long
like you said, if you stick with it you will probably get to
the end eventually.

Poem

So far
it has worked
by imagining you
in all the places I would
like you to be

*

this is the one I love.
he is not here
but the air is still warm
from where he
might have been

*

we have spent hours
circling each other
with words—thinly
vowelled embraces

*

how to translate these
words into silences
or the silences
into words

*

when I cannot fix you
behind my eyes
I carry your absence
like stars
on the blue roof

Rodnie and her bicycles

You and all your bicycles
coming down out of the sky like
wheeled birds, coat flaps
like wings
            I like to think of you and them
            pedalling through the sky
            each revolution a small turn
elsewhere.

You only ever wanted
one
you said, but they seemed to
seek you out
each morning dawned a new bicycle.

Now you have two in the shed
                a new blue one to ride
                one in the cupboard
                and the old black one which you put
out to pasture in the garden
in between the new plants.

I like to think of you
and the bicycles—all those possible
journeys waiting in cupboards
and behind old doors and,
in the night, you cycling out
through the garden,
your face shining like the spokes
from all your bicycles,
joy spinning in your face
like a wheel.

Paul and his ancestors

Paul is making
papier-mâché models
of his ancestors.

He shapes them in
paper and paste,
smooths over their
rough edges, gives
them each a sound
beginning in
chicken wire.

This way
they are of
manageable size.

He has put
a lightbulb inside
each person and
is considering
making them into
individual lamps or
an ancestral chandelier.

This way
his beginnings
light up the room like
so many global
revelations.
His ancestors gesticulate
wildly
they wave their arms
in the light.

Reading the body

I

Back lit
clipped
on the board
light goes
through you
shows you up in
black and white for
what you are—a
gather of bones
a curled frond
of a spine
lightly embraced by
that scooped-out
smoothness of hip
cavity whose bones
like open palms
seem to
offer themselves out
in a kind of
blessing.

II

Here are some pictures
of the body.

These are the bones
of my beginning.
They have stayed
with me like
true friends. They
have given
very fine
support.

See the way the
spine tails down
to a fine twitch

the way the ribs
are arms curved
in welcome

the way the hip bones
lie like an open book.

And finally

There would be
a series of paintings:

The Body as Ant
The Body as Incident
The Body as Intention
The Body as Masterpiece
The Body as Desire

The Body as Ant

The body
is small
and crawls
fast.
The body has
lots of
legs.
The body
lives underground
in a nest
and collects food.

The Body as Incident

The body
happens to itself
by itself.

The Body as Intention

The body
means well.
It means so well
that it falls
backwards
over itself.
The body
is full
of good
intent.

The Body as Masterpiece

The body
is a big body
is a work
of Art.
The body
is still
life.

The Body as Desire

The body
desires
a body
any body
just not its
own body.

Sophie travels backwards on the train

Sam

That summer Sophie found butterflies all through the house.
They were there, quiet on the window ledges
folded black and white against the skirting boards
no noise
one fitted perfectly, orange and red, into a window corner like stained glass.
The butterflies were silent
left breaths of colour in the house

Sophie couldn't bear to move them, even when the life left them and the small pieces of colour were blown by small sighs of wind onto the floor and into corners where mosaics slowly grew, piece by piece

It was as if they had come here to die—the last sanctuary before the colour left them.

❖

The storm had brought the sunflowers down.

Face down the big ones lay across the path, their heads buried in grass on the other side. Such a new view it must be, this green after blue, thought Sophie.

They must have been like flames falling from some altar, trailing light as they bent to earth, or like some heavenly catastrophe—the suns all falling from the sky.

Now there was sunlight strewn on the grass—each shaft a small death.

❖

She left them for two days before taking them out of the ground. She stepped over the ones across the path, careful not to disturb them and watched the grass start to turn yellow under the weight of the heads.

Because they were so heavy she had to break the stems before she was able to pull the roots from the ground.

They snapped like bones. The sound cracked loud across the day.

She broke them off and laid the stems with their heavy heads in a pile on the lawn—they were still tall, even though a quarter of their height was still in the ground.

Pulling the plants up from the ground was like uprooting small trees. The stems were the size of a child's wrist and the roots were firmly held. Sophie had to get the garden fork and lever them up from their hold.

They came, bringing huge moons of earth with them, creaking up from below.

They left huge craters, the stems leaning crazily at all angles, some crossing like swords—some ancient battlefield.

She crashed the roots against the side of the house to get the earth out and then one by one carried the plants to the compost pile. They lay like trees.

Then she went and sat by the pile of stems and flowers—their seed heads already whitening and the leaves brown, some of them, some of them still green.

She sat for a long time.

When it was very late and Sam asleep, Sophie got up.

She took the old garden shed door from its resting place against the house and carried it down to the sea. It took a while. The door was heavy and she had to carry it at her side, every so often stopping to change sides so her arms took turns at the load.

She left it leaning against the concrete sea wall, around a bit from where the fishing boats were moored. She could see Marco Polo, Michelangelo and Pisces sitting out on the water.

It was very still and the moon was up.

❖

The sunflowers took two trips. They were difficult to carry—heads heavy and the stems kept skewing off at all angles, thrown by the weight of the flowers. She carried them like children, cradled in her arms.

When she had laid the first pile on the door on the sand, Sophie went back for the next.

When she returned she laid the second lot on the first. There were about 20 stacked high.
Next she dragged the door down to the sea edge.

There were no waves. It was one of those silent nights where the water lay held between its edges.

The door floated easily. She walked with it. It floated quietly, a vague slip slip sound as it passed over the water.

She walked in until the sea lapped at her waist.
She was well clear of the boats, there was nothing around.

❖

Sophie set light to the end of the leaves and gave the door a gentle push. The flames caught at the dry plants, fled all the way up their stems and blazed on the dry heads. The pile flamed.

Nothing moved in the bay. If people watched from their windows they stayed clear, breathed their mist on dark glass and were silent.

The flowers burned over black water. Sophie stayed near until the last light went from the pile.

❖

When she bought the seeds, Sophie bought stakes as well. They were big stakes—six foot, 75 cents each.
She was anticipating great growth from these flowers—absolute height.

Later she was amazed to find that the flowers actually grew once they had bloomed.

They started small, almost silly on those huge stems and then rounded out until each day they were bigger than the last, those huge moon shapes watching out from their green posts.

❖

She sat out by the front steps and read
a complicated book about relationships
which worked its way backwards
somehow and you only really knew about
the beginning and the middle
when you got to the end—the further
you went, the more you knew
about what had gone before.

❖

In the book
he said
she said
she had another name
they had driven in the car for a very long time
he had his hand on her knee
she touched his shoulder every
now and again
he called her by her other name and sometimes 'babe'
it would all make sense in the end.

❖

Sophie watched a film about deaf and blind people.

Words were tickled into their palms,
they received them like communion—a gift
words for their eyes
they told about the hills' purple slant
their eyes heard the mountains' silent roar
in the blue as sharp as razors
Pass it on, thought Sophie.

In the park
the man made the tree with his hands
traced it onto the sky
he held the trunk like a fine friend
followed the branches out
and felt the leaves fall
out of sight.

❖

This was how she felt. She wanted to grasp hold of trees to know that they were trees, to find her own translations.

❖

Come on Sam
give us a go on the line

❖

Sophie wore dark glasses for a day. They had blue lenses and it was like being underwater.
Blue arms waving
a blue butterfly, like a fish, flies past

she wore red the world was on fire, gently
she walked into a fairy clock, floating like a small flame
it left a warm imprint, a mysterious tattoo on one breast

❖

In the shop window was the reflection of the bus she was on. Sophie knew she was somewhere in that image, that clear picture on the window, beyond the window, but she could not find herself, could not see herself, seated, near the back, in navy blue.

❖

Sophie saw a man in red socks lying on a park bench.
He had his head in the lap of a reading woman.
He had a paper over his eyes to shield him from the glare of the sun.
Sophie didn't think it was good for anyone to have the news that close.

❖

Sophie got on the bus.
It was like getting on the ferry—one of the ones that travelled between the islands
something to do with the light, she thought
and the wateriness of the night
and reflections.

The bus was parked on a lean in to the curve as though caught in some watery trough. It was like climbing aboard a boat and it rocked its way, riding the swell to the top of the hill.
Sophie saw oceans pass by the window
things swam in the blue

❖

It is because your heart beats
that you kiss me this way Sam
said Sophie

you can kiss me because of these
tiny jumps in your neck your
jaw, as the blood thumps through
small thunder

is it any wonder?
said Sam

❖

Sam tried to draw her
tried to sketch her outline
Sophie moved
    and moved
    and moved

can't get a line on me eh Sam

❖

Time to get out of here, Sophie thought
Time to scram.

❖

She said
here Sam, take this small round stone
hold it for a while
it is the very weight of me
put it in your pocket
carry it like a small prayer.

❖

Sam was always more interested in getting there—the moment of arrival
Sophie wanted all the things along the way—the process of getting there.

He never wanted to stop and when he got there, wanted to turn around and go back. A conquering of distance. The huge miles ran through with a shrug and he pointed things out as they passed them—look, see, there it is and then another distance, back to where they had come from
another track back
he could have kept on doing that.

But Sophie wanted all the arrivals. She arrived all the way there and all the way back.

Sophie travelled backwards on the train

Sophie travelled backwards on the train.
It was as if her whole life had been like that—a travelling away from, a speeding away from where she had been, facing it all the while as it got smaller and smaller until she almost forgot what it was, though she still carried the core of it with her, like a small fleck of light in her eye, while she travelled backwards, as if by default, to another location, situation.

The train sped her over the entire distance in reverse, while she kept the illusion of moving forwards, so it seemed she moved towards where she had come from while actually the distance spread behind.

And when she arrived, it would be with a sudden jolt—she would utter a small 'oh', pick up her bag and step out in this new place, see in wonder the distance travelled.

The speed, the sureness, the safety of the backward travel.

The leg

The cottage sat on the end of a finger of land which reached out into the bay. At high tide the sea stretched blue all around and it was as though the house was on an island, marooned out there.

When it was like this, Jack and Lily used to launch their dinghy from the front gate and head out for a morning's fishing.

Jack used to make jokes about opening the gate to let the big ones in and when Sophie was young, she had sat and waited to see the coloured fish line up for entry to the front garden.

Lily used to fish a lot, but as she got older it was harder for her to manage, having only the one leg. She still got around all right on her crutches but wasn't quite as agile anymore. She used to worry about slipping on the wet path. Jack used to say she was lucky to only have one leg to go stiff on her.

Lily knitted jerseys like the sea—waves of colour that had the sea in them. She used to send them off to the family—pieces of the ocean arriving unexpectedly in their mailboxes, washed up on their shores like bottles.

At nights, when Jack wanted to set a line, she'd sit up in bed by the open window, knitting her rows and flashing a torch signal to him every now and again.

He'd flash back three times when he saw her light.

Jack often went out at night—he wasn't really scared of anything, Sophie thought. He'd once worked for a circus and had the job of lying under the elephant's foot. Rinaldo the trainer would lead the elephant over to where he lay and while the crowd ooohed and aaahed, she would raise her right leg and place her foot, very lightly, on Jack's stomach. He lay very still. It was fine until the day she was upset by a noise and stood too close to Jack, brushing his ribs as she lifted her foot. It hurt terribly. He groaned and Rinaldo hissed 'shut up, shut up' and the crowd gasped and Jack had to lie there with three broken ribs, trying to be calm with the great grey foot resting on his stomach. Trying not to breathe, trying not to be there.

After that he had always measured everything by how it compared to lying under the foot of an elephant. Not much came close really, he said.

❖

The last time Sophie had visited was the time they'd picked tomatoes. She and Jack down in the huge garden wandering along the rows. They didn't speak much but she could hear him moving between the plants—their hot rustling gave him away.

Sophie put the tomatoes in her hat.

It's the little uns are the best, Jack said. Go for the little uns Sophie, they're good and sweet.

Uh huh, said Sophie.

They worked quietly along the rows.

Jack

mmmmm

What did happen to Lily's leg?

I'm never quite sure—she doesn't say and I don't ask. I don't even know if she knows herself, she was pretty young when it happened and probably they never told her why.

There was a silence.
Polio probably or somethin like that. Anyway what does it matter?

mmmm I spose.

When they'd picked enough, Jack and Sophie took the tomatoes over to the tap, washed them and laid them on the grass. Sophie sat and looked at them for a long time. Smooth red stones.

Only having one leg must have given Lily a curious outlook on life, Sophie thought. One based on a precarious sense of balance and a strong sense of the dangers of a wet path.

❖

Once when Sophie had got a taxi, the driver found out her name and said she'd once taken Lily somewhere (it must have been on one of their visits). Then the taxi driver said her granddaughter had just recently had her leg amputated because of cancer and she'd got worried about boyfriends and things because she was only young and thought they might be put off by her only having one leg, so her grandfather (the taxi driver's husband) told her he was going to write a book called *How to Make Love to a One-Legged Woman*. That had cheered her up a lot.

❖

When Jack went up to see Lily at the funeral parlour, Sophie stayed behind. She'd wanted to go, right up until that morning, but then couldn't imagine it. She thought she'd be looking for something, but didn't know what, so she stayed at home and waited until he came back and then asked about it.

Smooth. Jack said she looked smooth. Her face was much younger and he said he knew now where the photos of her when she was a young girl had come from. Funny thinking about your youth coming back to you when you died. All those wrinkles must've just been like a disguise.

Then, Sophie was glad she hadn't gone, but now she wondered. Probably better not to though—she would have wanted answers from her like: what about the leg?

❖

Once Sophie saw a man with one leg—he'd lost his left one. Sophie thought that if he and Lily had stood side by side the space where their legs should have been would be wide enough for a child to slip through, in the same way she and her friends had crept through the holes in the concrete lamp-posts up their street, slipped sideways through them, leaving a five or two cent piece on the top of the arch and always checking on the way home to see if it was there.

The cottage

In the cottage every sound is a definite sound. There are no quiet shufflings or silent steps.

The thunk of a lightswitch

The filling of a kettle with the sound stretched from the first dark splashes to a higher lighter tone as the level rises

Steps are solid and heard from heel to toe   she hears her feet fall in every room
No coming or going is a quiet one

Sound radiates out

But mostly it is the light switches—the solid flick of sound which decides yes or no, light or dark.

❖

Being in the cottage at night was like being in a forest.
Sophie wandered through the rooms   trees stood against the
walls   their branches shifted in the wind, blew against the door
frames, stretched unbroken across the bookshelves.

The room was full of trees
Sophie woke at night in the forest
then in the mornings it was the sea.

❖

In the cottage
the night comes in
the night goes out
there are trees around the walls
creepers on the floors

she is in the forest of her dreams
and the green leaves
suggest themselves

❖

When her mother was small, she and her sisters used to draw
houses on the sand
big houses
and they played in these houses, chased each other through the
rooms.

❖

Sophie stepped over people's names on the sand, names and the I loves—people's names twined in sandy embraces, lying there close until the sea licked down their spines and carried away all trace of them, erased all evidence, smoothed it down.

She wondered where all the names went.
Where did the houses end?
Was there a gathering place for all where the lovers stayed twined and the houses kept their rooms with the children running through or did the sea as it lifted them, intentionally swing them out on different waves, each letter parted from the others, to end up on a different beach, another set of waves in another ocean—all part of the great taking apart and the piecing together?

⁘

Sophie watched the waltz of the beach walkers

⁘

Swimming sometimes, when she put a foot down on sand Sophie felt a flounder flash away from under her step—smooth body like a plate.

⁘

There were two clues in the crossword that she particularly liked the sound of:
1. Bite out of the coastline, by the sound of it (5)
6. Bones going round and old ribbons (7)

⁘

On the track to the bay over the hill, Sophie stopped just past the first ridge. Looking across she could see the point on the top of the next rise where the scrub divided—a small crack in the green hill line—and she knew that soon she would stand in exactly that place and look back to where she stood now and remember it, almost remember the exact feeling of being here on this part of the track, with these particular trees, but not quite, it would stay just out of reach.

Then again, when she reached the part which first glimpsed the bay, she would look down at the whiteness of it and know soon she would be there on the sand, could almost see herself dotted there, or that speck in the surf, buffeted by the waves. Then she would be there and lie on her back in the water, looking up at the hill, realise her own vision.

She put herself there, then she was. She saw where she would be, on that ridge where the green split, and she was. Down there she floated amongst clean waves and yes, now she could feel the water cool on her skin.

⁘

Sophie looked down from the plane on fields—dark green and purple shapes laid down, it seemed, in some haphazard order. She tried to read the pattern of it—it seemed there must be some code to decipher, a way of reading, of piecing it together that would give a whole. Lead to a destination.

The clues — a fence line
— a gold splatter of hay, fallen like sunlight on a dark field
— trees grouped green in a corner, held by arms of wire on two sides
— thin worm trail of a plough traced lightly across dark ground

and through, across these odd traces, these random markings, Sophie tried to find a trail.

⁘

In the same way she looked at her own face in the mirror.

She saw: this line and this line and the thin trace of a furrow on her forehead and a slow curve etched lightly at the side of her mouth, which, when she smiled, jumped quickly to life then was gone again. And the tiny stars at the sides of her eyes that

scrunched and reached out sharply with thin fingers towards the side of her head.
These were her own shadows of trees, her own fencelines and magic traceries.

Where did these tiny signs come from, lead to?
Sophie tried to trace her life back through them.
Tried to follow the lines back to somewhere, trace the path she had taken, as though following clues that in the end would lead to a solving of the mystery that was her life.
This face of hers her own personal map.
You had to find your own way across the fields of clues,
make your own path.

Weighing up the heart

Always, there are our hearts
to consider.
They are most
precious to us.

*

The heart is a means
of description.
It will locate
the sentiment.
Speak up
small red thing.

*

The heart is
the deciding factor.
Wave your arms around
see the sky bloom.

*

The heart lives
as a steady witness
within the body.
We would hope
for a rigorous
sympathy
for the heart to
remember
the reliable place
in which it dwelled.

*

Always refer back
to the heart.
It is where
the world
began.

In love

This is a piece
to fit.
It is the piece
about her being
in love.
It should belong between the
piece of her before being
in love and the piece
of her after being
in love.
Instead it covers
everything.
The heart has no corners
and is stretched
to its limit.

Spring

In your dreams
I am always pale and
we are in Paris
which is just off the
end of Te Awamutu
I am learning to
water ski and can
say *pain au chocolat*
which somehow reminds
me of pain of death
—biting into soft
tragedies going for the
sweet centre which
confounds the plot.
Here it is time to take
a breath. We are now
on a driving holiday
somewhere north of
Waikanae   we forget
things and have to
drive back and forth
remembering
forgetting
and remembering
again.

Instructions for how to get ahead of yourself while the light still shines

If you have a bike, get on it at night
and go to the top of the Brooklyn Hill.

When you reach the top
start smiling—this is Happy Valley Road.

Pedal at first, then let the road take you down
into the dark as black as underground,
broken by circles of yellow lowered by the street lights.

As you come to each light
you will notice a figure
racing up behind.
Don't be scared
this is you creeping up on yourself.
As you pass under the light
you will sail past yourself into the night.

Working drawing

In the doorway is a woman
in a blue dress.
This is not the whole picture
there are some details
to be filled in, like
the furniture, the colour of
the vase on the table,
the space behind the woman
the space in front of the woman
the detail of any other persons
in the room, the detail of
the missing person who is
never found, and the detail of
her elbow—it being the clue
to the picture—the way it bends
that way in the light, the angle
giving some sort of a rough line
to go on with.

From behind the hedge

It sounds like one woman.
Her heels click across the road and every so often she says
something.
This is one woman talking to herself every now and again.

Or maybe there are two women.
One woman in loud shoes who every now and again comments
to another woman who is silent and wears soft shoes or maybe is
silent and is piggybacked across the road by the first woman so
as to give a false impression.

Or maybe the second woman is mute.
Maybe she taps softly on the first woman's shoulder in
answer—once for yes, twice for no, and maybe she stays
in the car while the first woman goes back and forth across the road.

Only one car door slams.
Is this because there is only one woman or because the mute
woman is tired?

Picture of the life

Here is a picture of the life.
The background is larger than
the foreground in places.
The land is a jumble sale of colour
hills unfold before other hills.

On the plain
two figures embrace.
They shake hands with their bodies.
pleased to meet you
pleased to meet you
oh I am so very pleased to meet you.

And from the sky, riding in on the rain,
come small pink frogs whose colour
can probably be explained by the word

ALBINO

the pink being the blood
leaping through the veins.

The movies

She wore a red dress.
She wore a blue dress.

The old house has
steps
up to the front door.

It opens.
It shuts.
The bell won't ring.

She faints at the sight
of flowers.

We think the nurse
is a bad egg.

A red hand
is danger.

Crocodile eyes
are good luck
and so is clover.

Even the fish
will remember.

The child is in danger.

You can smoke discreetly
in the library.

Sophie is the one
to watch.

Can I have the key
to the small trunk?

You look beautiful in red.
You look beautiful in blue.

Oh hold me close
Roberto.

It is hereditary.

Your wife was
my sister.

Your future is the present.

The child has become
a nun.

Let's go boating.

From the album

My mother and father
stand married.

They smile the most
beautiful of smiles.
My father with the thinnest
of faces
and my mother's dark
eyes shining.

The corner of my mother's
wedding dress lifts
in the breeze
and her veil fills
like a sail
gently steering her
towards us.

*

1.

Here is a picture of the eldest
one in her early days.
She has that look
on her face
as she half crouches, half kneels
with one knee
tucked up under.

2.

Here is that big
blond beautiful
woman as a small
round girl with hair
as straight as pins.

She holds her head to one side.
She is trying to understand
the question.

3.

The two of them bury
the smallest one
in the sand.
Only her head
sticks out.
She shyly rides the journey
horizontally, sits up
at the station and brushes
the sand from her lap.

*

A picnic.
Tartan bermuda shorts
togs slung in a tree
lanky kids with damp hair.
Skateboards made
from bits of wood
and old skate wheels.

There would have been a barbecue
and a ball somewhere
and probably a bat.

Endless days.
Of course.

Holidays at Golden Bay.
A small bach on the beach.
Photographs show us proudly holding fish by their tails or naked
by the upturned dinghy with the shore curving, like memory,
behind.

One year our young teacher came to visit. We stood on our heads to impress her. Her sister was engaged to a man in France. He had been in a car accident and lay badly injured, unconscious in hospital.
It was so romantic we could hardly stand it.

Dad caught an enormous fish off the wharf but it got away.
This big.   This big.   This big.

At home, a girl called Shona moved in to the house over the back. She had white holy communion shoes. We locked her in the shed.

One christmas our mother went quiet.
Dad took the three of us shopping.
We had our photograph taken on the front lawn of our friends' house looking uncomfortable in our best dresses, worried by our mother's silence which followed us across the road and stood by us as the camera clicked.

Barefoot at school
warm concrete
heaven.

Wanting.
Wanting to look like a girl called *Laura*.
Wanting to be able to run like a *gazelle*.

*

THE WATCH

The watch I carry in my pocket was my father's. A gift on his 21st birthday. It is a big-faced solid watch—ROAMER, 17 JEWELS, SWISS MADE, SUPER-SHOCK. The even numbers are very round and in place of the odd numbers are the shapes of slender arrow heads. In the photographs this watch accompanies my father through his life. In the wedding picture of him and my mother I can see the winder edging out from under the sleeve of his dark suit. My mother's hand rests on his arm. Holding on to his other arm is

his mother. To their right stands my grandfather—in the window behind there is a woman's hat and it looks as if it has just blown off his head. I realise that all the people in the photograph—except for my mother and father—are now dead. My two grandmothers, my grandfather and two smiling young men.
The watch is solid on his wrist as my father holds me—a tiny child almost covered over by his big hands. It is there as he balances my sister Jane on his shoulders and again as he holds Wendy against his knees.
This watch is my father as a young man still new to the world. Now he has a new watch and I have this old one. I carry in my pocket my father aged 21, his lean face ticking through the years.

*

My grandmother is held forever in a photograph taken. One of the last ones. She sits in a car outside our old house—the window is open slightly and she is low in the seat. You can just see her face framed by the window and the top of one of her crutches propped at the side of the seat.
She looks out at the camera.
I have her there forever.
When I dream of her it is this photograph that I dream.
Always her looking out at me through the window.

The day before her funeral my auntie gave us a photograph of her when she was a young girl and still had both her legs. She stands on some stairs which curve away behind, one hand on the banister, still, in a dark velvet dress. She looks out from the stairs at the camera—her face solemn, firm on two legs.

I have another photograph of a young girl in a velvet dress. It is an old picture I found in an antique shop. The girl has a dark velvet dress on and beads and on both her legs she has long white socks and shoes. Sometimes I think this is my grandmother. She also has a bow in her hair. Sometimes I think all young girls with velvet dresses and two legs must be my grandmother.

*

She still wore her wedding ring, even though they'd not been married for a long time for years. Johnny ran away one day with Zelda from next door—my grandmother's best friend and mother of the children my father and his sister played with. They ran away to Rarotonga where he was an engineer and she marvelled at hibiscus.

*

My grandmother reserved a face of stone for any mention of my grandfather and he in turn reserved silence.
These reservations they held in the hotel of their ex-marriage for 30 years—from the day my grandfather left to the day my grandmother died.

*

Our friends across the road had

an attic
a dolls' house
a trailer
tekupons   what?
teakupons   what?
tecupons, teacoupons, tea coupons   oh

a kettle, the soundness of a kettle, not a jug. A silver
kettle with a red switch which you pushed in when you wanted
the water to boil and, when it had, the kettle whistled
and the red switch clicked out

a pressure cooker
gem irons for ginger gems
a sifter—cylindrical—you pumped the handle and the silver
blades turned over and over like a mill.

They knew about cooking.

They were always peeling spuds
and going down the back garden to pull up carrots
or pick sweetcorn
or silverbeet

or raspberries

and they had secat*eu*rs

and they never followed recipes very closely

sultanas   just throw some in
how many?
what does it say?
a cup
well just chuck them in
that many?
that'll do

Phil used to hold the wooden spoon right down by its head and beat and beat and flick her long thick red hair like flames away from her eyes.

They cooked and baked in a haphazard manner
and it was always miraculous

they lived in a desirable chaos of six children and a haphazard baking and cooking and gardening and tinkering with cars—the boys—and always a putting on of the spuds.

They had a grandmother with hair so long she could sit on it.
We saw the photographs.
We had a grandmother with one leg.
That door, that cupboard, what's in there?
That's where our grandmother lives.
Do you keep her in a cupboard?
No stupid, it's a whole other house through there, she's got her own house.

And trees.
And leaves from the trees.
In autumn they reached the back garden of our friends over the road and would get in between the silverbeet and the corn and cover the grass.

On windy nights they filled the street.
The man next door swept and swept and we swept and bagged and raked and tried to keep the piles under control but never could.

In spring the lawn would be covered with the beginnings of elm trees whole forests of tiny trees—and we would mow them down, but not before marvelling at how these became
those, those giants which dominated our view.

In spring the sight of fresh leaves first thing.

And the same trees at the house next door.
But they trimmed theirs, cut off all the branches that stretched towards their house, leaving them half trees, with a trunk and branches one way.

We had a swing there—a huge swing which arced out and easily reached the fence between our two houses. We spent our childhoods immersed in the rhythm of swinging, of up and out.

*

SONG FOR THE PARENTS

They love each other
like crazy

like crazy
they love each other

crazy like they love each other
each other they love like crazy.

(Repeat)

The boyfriends

The boyfriends all love you but they don't really know how.

They say it is tragic that you will not be together for the rest of your lives. You will not be together for the rest of your lives because they are lone spirits and you are a nice girl.

Because your father is a lawyer and because they like to think they come from the wrong side of town, they say you will marry a young lawyer. Someone nice, someone stable, someone able to provide you with all the things you need and are accustomed to, not a rogue, not an adventurous spirit like themselves. Not someone who is destined to the lone life.

They say it will be all right for you. You will be very happy, they can tell. It will all work out for you. You will find a young lawyer, or a young lawyer will find you and you will get married and be very happy.
This is what you want, of course.
They say you are made for happiness, anyone can see that.
You will be very happy, you'll see.

They imagine their own sorrow when the day finally comes. They tell you about this. They imagine seeing you in town with your new young lawyer. He will have his arm around your shoulders. You will be looking happy. He will be looking happy. You will both be looking very happy. They will look on and feel tragic about it not working out, about the impossibility of the great love. Because yours is the great love. The true love. Oh yes. But it cannot work. The great love never works. The true love is doomed to fail.

You suspect they have seen too many westerns with too many cowboys riding off into too many sunsets.

In the end of course, you leave him. There isn't really much choice. He is unhappy. Very unhappy. It is not all that romantic. When you see him in the street you often cannot speak. You just look at each other. You both cry a lot in public places. Other people find this embarassing and so do you.

He says   please come back.
He says this is the worst thing that has ever happened. And it is.
Please he says. Please.

But you can't. Because it would be going back to leaving him. You prepared yourself to leave him for years. It took such a long time.

It took years of listening to him leaving you, knowing that he wouldn't.
All that leaving.
All that is left is the leaving.

Bus stop

1.

At the bus stop we are fascinated by everything.
Trees on the hill above
the wind in them
everyone else coming from all directions, diving out from streets around the hillside, emerging from cars, coming up the road, all with the bus stop in mind.
We cluster around it waiting fresh from our beds waiting beside others fresh from their beds everyone fresh and clean and ironed and wind blown gathering their clothes around them.
And we are interested in everything—the coat worn by the man and the shoes worn by the woman and the falling down socks of the young girl with the beautiful face.
And when the nice woman tells the young man he has left his parking lights on we are overjoyed with the drama of it all, crane our necks, follow him down the road with our eyes, want to clap a little, say   what grace   what style.

2.

Look out all around you
the trees grow before our very eyes
turn into forests we could get lost in.

Having done that, having lost
the bus stop and the others waiting at it
we would then be alone in the forest
wandering about
and would be grateful, joyful, at stumbling across
a fellow passenger
we would discuss our most vital needs with these strangers
saying   *food*   *water*   in reverential tones
and we would ask the most
important things of each other
like—I have cut my hand, please, would you bind it for me.

Make sure

Make sure you fall in love with a man who you know will survive
in the bush.
This way, when he is three nights overdue from his trip and the
search and rescue team is out looking for him and the helicopter
has been called back because the weather is closing in and they're
interviewing you on television in a close-up camera shot, asking
you what you think his chances are—hoping you will cry and
your lip will tremble—you can look them straight in the eye and
say you know he will be all right, he has had plenty of experience
and he knows what to do, he was carrying plenty of food and
warm clothing and he is strong.
Even if he is hurt, you know he will be all right.
He's a fighter, you'll say. He won't give in.
But the weather is closing in, you must be worried, they'll ask.
You keep your resolve. He will be all right, you say.
I know he will.

The bathers

Les Grandes Baigneuses—Cézanne
(begun about 1898 or 1899 and finished 1905)

Left for eight years amidst
the intense green and blue
of trees   pleased Cézanne
abandoned them in such a
pleasurable landscape.
Bodies slanted towards trees,
water, a dog asleep on the
ground. They sighed, over those
eight years, talked amongst
themselves quietly, each morning
a small *ah* of pleasure
at the day, wondering if
today . . . for eight years
until the trees grew thick
with colour, the lake
darkened and their bodies'
cool formation fixed
beside the admiring water.

Cast in order of appearance

Best to be
the   GIRL IN BED   in
the movie. He gets up
brushes a light hand across
your sleepy breasts, you ask
will I see you again?
and he says, as he pulls on
his shirt *no* then you say
as he's going out the
door *you've got great*
hands and he smiles a little
and exits, leaving you
alone in your room above
the café where the neon sign
flicks information onto your
wall. And it suits you. You
lie for a bit. The rest of
the movie is all yours. You're
left to dress in private, to
go downstairs and have coffee
in the café before meeting up
with the   MAN WITH SAUCE BOTTLE
who doesn't appear until later
but gets a laugh and might
be remembered. You won't
be, unless it's days later
in an idle moment and by
that time you'll be miles
away, on holiday with friends
out on the lake in a boat
taking in the trees.

Tourists often stop

Tourists often stop and take photographs of the red hot pokers at
the bottom of our drive.
They get up close to the splendid display, focus, bend
their legs slightly and brace for the snap.

Japanese men take the photographs home and show them to
their friends.

This is the woman I fell in love with over there, they say.
Unfortunately her mother is dying and she cannot leave her.

American women take the photographs home and show them to
their friends and say: this is a man I fell in love with over there.
We were on a bus tour together. It was his second time and he
showed me all the sights. He was a real dag. We had a real fun
time. His name is Reg. We are planning an underwater wedding.

Man looking at trees

Over the road in the park there is a man looking at trees. He walks around looking up at them and when he is finished looking at one he turns away, only to find another, so he heads on over for a closer look, walks around it, head back, gazing upwards. He might be thinking about how beautiful are the trees. How wondrous nature is. He might be bringing god into it. He might be thinking words like *height* and *girth* or he might just have green on his mind. He is wondering about these trees. He might be thinking about how good it would feel to chop these trees down, about the feel of the blade against the trunk. It might be blue he has on his mind and he might be thinking about how good the sky would look if there weren't all these trees in the way.

Man with a mower

There is a man sitting on a tractor mowing circles in the park. In the middle of the area he is mowing there is a group of people wandering about. Five of them. They move in a bunch. One of them holds a piece of paper which they all consult every so often. They stand for a while and look at the paper then they look up and around them and sometimes someone draws a line in the air with their finger and they all look at it, then look back at the paper again. Then one starts moving and the others follow. The grass is quite long and rather wet so they lift their legs high as they walk.
The men wear grey suits, the hems of which are getting damp from standing in the grass. They walk as though crossing a river, going from stone to stone. One of the men wears a lemon tie. One of the women has on a lemon outfit and red shoes. She and the man may be involved or it may merely be a coincidence. The women's legs are also getting wet as they move around in the grass in the park. They stand and look and study and point and look and move on. And all this time the man on the tractor is mowing his circles around them, getting closer and closer so the grass on the outside where he has been, is shorn and the people stand in the long grass like an exhibit.
The tractor is noisy. The people in the grass must have to talk loudly when the mower passes on its way around them. The man on the tractor wears ear muffs. He is thinking about a mince pie. He is thinking about Dolly Parton. He is thinking about the snake tattooed on his buttocks and the way it wriggles as he walks.

A woman walks

A woman coming up the road walks as though she is always looking around a corner. The expectant angle of her body suggests that something is about to happen. She is obviously a woman with a history of *events*—here she is prepared for the next one lying in wait for her.

Friends stay with us

Friends stay with us. They sleep on the fold-out bed.
In the morning Louise gets out of bed still wearing her clothes.
She gets up early because she cannot sleep and goes for a walk in the park.
She walks around and looks at the statues. The man between the cannons. The woman with her hand on one breast. The man sleeping in the band rotunda.
She comes back from her walk and gets straight into bed and sleeps. Tim is quite used to this. She often goes to bed half dressed, or wakes half dressed, always prepared for a journey or having just returned from one.

Tree like a tree

In one corner of the courtyard there is the suggestion of a tree. If the tree had branches it would be tall and leafy and birds would sing in it, but the branches have been chopped and from the trunk come short flat-topped stumps, stopped in mid-air.
There is the feeling of a tree going places. The sky around it makes way for the possibility of branches. The word almost is in the air.

Cars in our driveway

Cars turn in our driveway.
All day cars slow on their way up the hill, turn into our driveway then reverse out and go back the way they came.
All day we think we are getting visitors. When we see a car nose in we rush to put the jug on to make a cup of tea for our guests.
Our hospitality excels itself.
There are single motorists, friends, couples and couples with families.
When we see children in the back seat we worry—do we have enough food in the house?

Saturday and Sunday

Every Saturday and Sunday a man comes to sit in the courtyard. He reads the newspaper leaning against the brick wall. The cats warn of his coming—one by one they look around, then, startled, run under the verandah.
We know the man is still there by the paper twitching above the wall.
Sometimes there is his hand turning a page.

Trees in America

American tourists walk down the road and look at the trees in the park.
Wow. Wow. I can see them say.
There are no real trees where they come from. In America they pay people to dress up in outfits with trunks and branches and as you walk past the trees say 'howdy' and shake your head.

Near misses

There are many near misses on the street in front of our house. Cars turn, cars speed up, cars pull out. No one looks. We watch from the window. We cry *oh* and *look out* and *so close*. All day we raise our hands to our heads in horror. Each day we wake up younger than the day before. Years are being taken off our lives.

Nearly Mrs

Men propose to women in the park outside the window. Sitting under trees they say *will you marry me*. Every day there are some very nearly Mrs.

Someone plants a tree

Yesterday someone planted a tree in the middle of the courtyard. When we looked out the window late in the afternoon we saw a tree we were sure we were seeing for the very first time. The ground around the base of the tree looked a little disturbed, but whoever planted it had been careful to put the turf back so it looked as though actually the tree might have been growing there all along and we'd just never noticed it. We were sure this was a new tree, but then again . . .

Every day now

New trees and bushes appear outside our window every day now. These trees don't grow there, they just arrive. We are now not sure which have been there a long time and which are new. How many days has that tree been there? we ask each other. When did that climbing rose arrive? Now we question the existence of even the oldest trees. That oak, we say, how long has that been there? I don't remember that palm being there yesterday. And what about that big one in the corner? And that tree over the road—how can we be sure that didn't just come down in the last shower?

Two gardeners

Two gardeners come and sit in the courtyard every day about
noon. They sit on one of the green seats—the one facing the
window—and they smoke a joint.
One gardener is tall and one is short.
At first they both had long hair and beards and wore jeans,
Swanndris and boots. Then one day the shorter one came with
a woollen hat on and no sign of hair beneath it. A week later the
taller one appeared with his hair cropped close to his head. A few
days later, as if in answer, the shorter one arrived in shorts, with
his hat off, revealing a shaved head. The taller one followed by
clipping his beard and next, the shorter one came with no beard at
all, but his hat back on.
What a performance. We watch and applaud. This is men
changing before our very eyes.

Waiting shelter

1.

He remembers me standing in a doorway
stopping to talk to him over my shoulder
but not turning my body towards him.

I remember him as a man on a roof or
a man swimming, as a man asleep with
the next door dog's loud dreams travelling

over the fence and in the window. Look out
the window and there is a woman moored
offshore—a raft children swim out to

and play on. She has a different address
no longer 'care of', but still, the need for
such care to be taken. How precious it

is. How it needs to be cared for. There was
a house they moved in and out of but never
together. How far we have come from

closeness and how we remember it. The
turning away, the angling of bodies in
and out of doorways   oh how she

remembers and how he remembers. Another
house she lives in. Dull body of a moth
thudding against the blinds. A red car

in the driveway. It comes and goes. Harriet
says she gets confused between yesterday
and tomorrow. Was it the weekend yesterday?

she yells from bed. No. Why not? Sun
in the window in the morning. Shadows of
leaves on paper blinds. Children up the street

say hello. Cats in ecstasy. Here it is
now, while over there memory presses
close. A kiss betrays the present. A raft

swings on its moorings. Things to be paid
for. Next door is a family from Afghanistan.
They escaped at night across the border—

parents and seven children. Now they live
in Herne Bay and the eldest daughter drives
the car without her licence, stalls all the way

up the road, mounts the kerb then the traffic
islands, is all over the place but never stops
being intent on getting where she is going to.

2. **Ginny and the Taj Mahal**

Bean rolls on the beach with Ginny.
But first, her inside laughing about
Anne trying to seduce Ed in the hotel

room afrer visiting the Taj Mahal.
She'd like to see them here at
Cheltenham. She'd like to see them

at the Bakers Oven buying twenty
cakes. We're here on the beach being
seduced by warm air. Both of us

waiting, lying in wait for Ed,
waiting to see what his next move
will be. He might be a goner, but

he might not. We'll have to see.
He'll have to see. Meanwhile the
clouds have come over. Rangitoto's

dark crown caps the harbour, gulls
interrupt the air and we swim
Ginny in green togs, hair red above

the waves. She whoops and disappears,
pale legs surprise, soles of her
feet kick up against the sky.

3.

In the letterbox a card saying
'We're Very Interested in Your Home'.
But it is not her home. And she does

not have a child, even though, also
in the letterbox, she finds a pink
baubled hair elastic. She takes these

things inside to think about. Homes
and children. Things too large for
letterboxes. On her way up the steps

she finds a clump of seaweed and a
pair of swimming goggles tangled in
the red water fuchsia. She picks them

up. Takes them inside. Leaves them by
the answerphone and starts the ironing.
But they are not her clothes.

4.

So many children. Their signs. Chalk
drawings on the footpath—a cat, a boat,
I love you Izzie, noughts and crosses,

arrows leading to the top of the street.
Harriet wants to wear two dresses to
school. A man stands in the doorway. He

comes and goes. At the park in the
mornings she keeps running into
someone who is never there. Footprints

his signature. In them shine the silver
coins of spider webs. He comes towards her
and they pass at every step but never meet.

5.

Camels tethered to trees in the park.
An elephant cools off under the motorway.
Pressed against a large bush is a miniature

piebald horse. Sam plays golf with a lawyer
who was fired from his last job for
repeatedly somersaulting the reception

desk. Harriet says jelly is the perfect
food for adults. Someone else says something
but she isn't sure what it is. The boat he

is building in the back garden gets bigger by
the day. There is no way out for it but over
the top of the house. So he prays for rain.

6.

How you remember people. To remember
them as well as they remember you.
To remember them with abandon. To

abandon remembering them. Which is
better? or worse? Rooms and rooms
and always people moving in

and out of them. Love,
love, a knock on the door. A
heart murmur to remember you by.

7.

An arrangement he makes. Removes
himself and leaves her on a verandah
looking out across the bay. Down there

she can see, clearly, a red boat with
two people in it. One leans across to
kiss the other—two figures closing

in. Two as one, then two. On the line
bees cling to her blue shirt. Their
grip on a precarious sky. She makes

her own arrangement. Red roof, blue sea,
green boat passing over it. The distance
from the verandah to the red dinghy one

of faith's blind leaps. Two figures close
in. One leans across to kiss the other.
Clearly. Or is it just to bait the line?

8.

His body she misses. More than a
stone's throw from here. A lifetime
away, his long limbs lap at the

shore of her skin. She remembers
him well. At the back of her mind
is his mouth, soft as water.

9.

This house she finds herself in. Men work
on it. Outside, too, men dig up the footpath
camp in a caravan called *Ginty's*. One spends

whole days lying on the bridge over the motor-
way, watching cars slide up the valley,
hammering. Repairs. The damage done. Love's

disrepair. Where do they find themselves?
And how? In his backyard of trees he dreams
of fast-growing grass, skims the lawns nightly

feels the crush of the soft green carpet
underfoot. She lives in the house on the mend.
A boy comes to stay. He is the brother she

never had. He reads books she has never heard
of—*Monsters in Orbit* and *The Weird of the*
White Wolf. In the mornings she runs around a

park accompanied by elderly Chinese people
who shuffle in their grey clothes in the early
light.

10.

Roadworks and the road works again.
Men with shovels dig down deep. One
shows her blurred photographs of his

grandfather who was a cyclist in the
Boer War. He had his spokes shot out.
The grandfather is circled in red pen

and has a red arrow pointing to his
head. The famous bicycle is circled
too. It is difficult to tell exactly

what is going on. There is also a photo-
copy of a train ticket. Whose ticket
and where? no one knows, but the *Ginty's*

man wonders. A rose arrives. But not
from him. No message. She busts it up.
He sends her photographs—their

ancestry. She sits under a sign
Waiting Shelter. He stands in the company
of a chipped angel and headless birds

and again, wearing a dune like a turban
the sea a robe tossed about his shoulders.
Here too is his son, jumping boy high

in the sky. These pictures come from
the other country that was their life.
A foreign language close to their own.

An advertisement in a magazine reads:
. . . we can not tell you
whether Martin Kemp will
marry Sally Meryl in the
eightieth episode, but we are
sure that at the end of the
story you will speak English
as well as they do, or even
better . . .

II.

Language slips by. Washing in the
drier sounds like letters falling
through the door. At the Post Office

everyone speaks with an American
accent. A Chinese man wants envelopes.
The man serving has a bad stutter.

Her father rings from Austria, says
it is all Mozart and the Sound of
Music. He is off to Lake Wolfgang to

put his feet up. He is depressed
because the whole world is the same.
Everywhere he goes there are lakes,

hotels, churches, castles, towers,
boats for hire and historical facts.
Across the other side of town a man

is receiving roses and mistakenly thinks
they are from her. In another country
a man takes his life out onto a lake

and sails around in it. Sightseeing.
Astonished and at the same time
blinded by what he sees.

12.

This house with the sea out the window
boats moored on the walls and boats moored
out the window on the jawline of the

harbour. Below, the city shaken out like
a tablecloth. The eyes' picnic.
Sea sweeps in, an arm moving across a

sheet at night. The house a ship
moored on the edge and it in turn their
mooring. Upstairs and downstairs they ring each other

up. She dials the number of the older woman,
hears the phone ring, follows her footsteps
across the floor and hears, yes, her voice

on the other end. They talk with only the floor
between them. *Did you see the moon last night?*
I almost rang you up. Her husband built

boats. Their pictures line the walls. His
first boat. Their yacht in a race. The two
of them sailing. Him leaning out, looking

back. She waits for the grief to pass
like a ship slipping silently out. Cranes
spin against the hillside. They both wait.

For a departure. An arrival. The house
moored in a bay of waiting. Day climbs in
the window. Waterfront buildings lively

with light. This house poised on the edge
of sail.

Overseas

For years she has listened to people talk about overseas. For years, over dinner, someone has been saying *St Peter's Square* and everyone at the table has nodded. After some years she also began to nod because the square and other places had become so familiar she felt she had been there. She could now recount her own stories of overseas. When someone said 'that café in Paris, the one painted red inside, to the left of the Arc de Triomphe' she could chip in, with all confidence, saying 'no, no, it's on the right, two down from the place that sells the wonderful bagels'.

⁂

She has an aunt who cuts plastic New World supermarket bags into strips and knits them into sunhats with large brims. Once she made her husband—now dead—a hat from Coca Cola cans opened out, with the edges crocheted together in red wool. This same aunt has a fondness for old Sunlight liquid containers—the large ones. She cuts the top three-quarters of the fronts out and constructs nativity scenes inside with Mary, Joseph, baby Jesus and the three wise men in their yellow manger.
Would this happen in Paris?
Or Rome?

⁂

In Wellington she can buy coffee and have it ground in a machine called CLIMAX.

⁂

In Pamplona in Spain they run with the bulls. She knows this from reading James A. Michener.
Her 60-year-old aunt once wrestled a huge bull over a fence after it had gored her husband. Her advice, after further reading on the subject, is:

> If you are being charged by a bull, don't run, and don't eyeball it. Stand side on so you don't appear as a large obstacle.

❖

Photos from America

Here's Phil, Nick, Me, Susie, Guy and Steve

and this is Randy, Gary, Me, Susie, Bud and Jolene eating tacos in Mexico.

❖

Violet—her grandmother—writes to her from Greymouth. She sends photographs of old movie stars saying they are photographs of her in her younger days. Here is a picture of me and here is a picture of my first husband Jeremiah. He was a dashing young man with a temper as quick as a rattlesnake, she says of Clark Gable. I left him after he gambled away all our money. After that I went on a long journey where I ended up doing acrobatics on the back of a horse in a circus in Madrid. It was after I returned home that I met your grandfather who was a true gentleman and never did me wrong.

Here is a picture of a man I met in Madrid. We had what you young people would call a 'wild time'. The music, the dancing, the wine, the starry nights . . . oh, it makes me weep to remember.

Here are the gardens in Paris where my first husband Jean-Paul proposed to me, writes Violet. He was very handsome and he gave me a rose. Alas, our life together was cut tragically short when he was drowned in a boating accident. I felt robbed of love. It was then that I decided it was dangerous to marry foreigners. They die and leave you in ways you are unaccustomed to.

❖

In a bookshop in the central city a man orders books on the Beatles:

The Beatles in Tokyo
The Beatles in Holland
Dark Horse: Secret Life of George Harrison
and *Four Ever—Die Geschichte Beatles*, in which the text is in German but the pictures are in English.

❖

She reads in an overseas magazine:

> The Shopping Bag is the tip
> of the iceberg . . . the essence of
> image . . . the haiku.

So this is how they view it over there.
Writing as carrier bag. The poem as shopping
trundler. The short story as overnight bag.
The novel a leather suitcase with wheels for
ease of movement.

❖

She knows that all young French women are tall, thin and have short black hair. They are independent and wear white cotton underpants which come up to their waist.
When they become older they are still thin but their hair is long and blond and pulled up into a sophisticated yet casual roll at the back. They have a husband who knows about cooking and two beautiful children, yet they are often disappointed.

❖

Her cousin bought the New York State and the Chrysler buildings in Wellington, years ago.
The Chrysler building he assembled in Wellington but it was recently moved up the coast to Waikanae.
The New York State he made one cold winter in Tokyo and now it's in London in the main room of his Kensington apartment. It's lit up at night and you have to be careful not to knock it over as you go through the door.

❖

Because she is alone she is almost as popular as Michelangelo's *David*.
Families all over the world have her in their holiday snaps. She just seems to get in the way, the only one not smiling, looking away.

I was sure we only had three children, couples say to each other. Who is this? friends of families all over the world ask. Oh, that's just someone we met, they say: my sister's stepdaughter from her husband's third marriage, the mother of Brian's illegitimate children. That, they say, is the daughter we never had. We found her in Florence and she recognised us instantly.

We will we do

From behind the curtains
of Germany came
the family.
My father's grandparents
walking the streets of
Hamburg thinking
New Zealand
New Zealand
My mother's family
stepping out for
London then
Australia then
New Zealand
intersecting at a
church dance   he
tall blond and
gaunt   she dark
dark hair dark
eyes in a new
dress   may I
have the pleasure
we will   we
do they said.

*

Where did our family come from?
They were Danish
               German
from an annexed part of Germany
Schleswig-Holstein
Danish
German
Danish
German

There is an isle of Bornholm
and a large furniture store with our surname.
So they say.
Are our relatives, distant though they are,
involved in the business of chairs and lounge
suites and 'occasional tables' and tables for
dining and tables for all occasions in Germany?

All our childhoods a chorus of young girls' voices
a chorus to skip by: German
                                    Danish
                                    German
                                    Danish
                                    German

*

They might have been married
in St Michaelis Church with its
golden scrolls and
angels   her dress wall-
white   if he half closed his
eyes all he saw was her face
smiling at him saying
I do
                yes
      I do

Or in Katharinenkirchhof
down a street called
Grimm.   She came here tall
in her white dress to this
church with half a golden
spire, high vaulted white
ceiling with gold
stars, coloured light
firing in from the windows
saying   I do
I do   in all the colours

light picked her up
carried her ablaze
to him.

St Jacobi
clock on the spire with a star
and the moon on its hands.

*

Krempdorf, near Hamburg
one of the kick-off points
for the family
long ploughed fields strike out
for the horizon

'Krempdorf has no records.
It is very small.
It is a village.
Krempe is a town. They
will have records.

But not of Krempdorf
because it is a
village. Not a town.
It is very small.
It is nothing.'

*

This road they passed along
on their way to
the village.
The wind is very bad
today   yes
yes, he nods, yes

*

From the Register of Births at Krempe
Members of two families with the same name:

1771 Timm
1773 Metta
1776 Johann
1779 Albert
1780 Metta
1782 Peter
1786 Clause
1788 Cicilia
1792 Anna
1802 Silja
1804 Totgeburt
1806 Albert
1808 Carsten
1809 Totgeburt
1809 Johann
1811 Hinrich
Magdalena
1813 Tim
1815 Cocilia
1818 Abelona
1823 Albert
1829 Cathrine Margareta
Anna Magdalena
1831 Peter Otto
1833 *Hinrich*
1834 Metta Magdalena
1835 Catharina
1836 Anna
1837 Anna Wiebke
1838 Catharina
1839 Claus
Johann Otto
1840 Hans Hinrich
Anna
1842 Magdalena
Maria Margretha
1843 Johann
1845 Johann
Abelona
1846 Abel
1847 Metta Abeline
1849 Johann
Margaretha
1852 Abeline
1853 Peter
1857 Johanna Luise
1870 Wilhemena Cathrine
1871 Hinrich Hans
1874 Johann Hinrich

*

'A family Bornholdt still here,
see, Bornholdt and Hinrich too
is his name. They have been married
for 50 years. They have a golden
wedding.'

Into a house which smells of apples.
Bowls of potatoes on the kitchen floor.

But this is not your family.
Yours is long gone.

Later at the buro
we drink coffee and eat
plum cake beside the registers
of births and deaths, look at
an atlas and you point
to New Zealand. *Oh*
says Frau Bear *many miles*
on the other side.

*

Put on your best dress and go to visit
your great great grandparents who are not
expecting you.

The family comes through
the fields to meet you.

Bertha in a red dress.

Abeline on her way to marry
carries flowers.

Margaretha lies in the grass
by the barn dreaming of Frank
in Trittau

Hinrich on his way to sell
cigars in Hamburg. You pass him
on the road.

*

A woman walks past with a wheelbarrow
full of sweet peas.

Next to the station a man mulches
apples with slow strokes of

the shovel then adds them to his dark
compost heap.

At the station a man and teenage boy sit.
I ask about the train to Hamburg.
Soon, they say.

The man pats the ground beside him.
I sit down.
He drinks beer, points at the young boy and says
English.
Both work in Krempe, live at
Itzehoe. The boy works in admin
which sometimes is not so good, and the man
he is a carpenter.
He used to be a sailor—Liverpool, Jamaica,
until he had his accident. Holds up his right
arm and waggles his little finger—the only
one left on his hand.

*

Pass your great grandfather Hinrich on his way to work
at the Pipitea Wharf Freezing Company, dreaming of
Landunsbrucken, St Pauli,
of the farm at Krempdorf, his mother stewing apples,
his father ploughing
dreaming of the attic room above the grocer's shop in Hamburg
where he lived,
where he was when his mother died
'where he was when she fell down'.
In the business of groceries and cigars
where he was when he married Emma at St Pauli
stepping through the blackened ruins of the cathedral
the spire black as night against
day sky
to New Zealand
to where you remember them
in a dark room
with a canary.

Here's Hinrich
just arrived in New Zealand aged
seven. He's lost for words.
Language abandons him in this
new country. You in turn
flounder among unfamiliar sounds
in Germany—over your head in
a tongue not your own.

*

Hinrich abandons New Zealand as
a young man and returns to Germany,
though later to return.
You also abandon.

*

Here's Hinrich as a child
in Hamburg feeding swans by
the Binnen Alster.

*

The long arms of the family rest
along the shoulders of the world.

*

Meet your grandfather Henry Eugen (Harry)
as a young boy on the Oriental Terrace
zig zag. He's on his way home to
McIntyre Avenue after swimming in
the salt water Te Aro baths, laughing
and laughing, running home to tell
his brothers about the octopus getting in
to the pool through the pipe.

Running down Majoribanks Street on a day in 1912
on his way to work as a lolly boy at the Opera House.

On his way to grow up and leave school at 13
start his mechanical and general engineering

apprenticeship. Eager. Runs towards
the bridges he will build. Spends five years as
an apprentice and one as a journeyman
emerges at the start of the Orongorongo
Tunnel in 1922 and begins work.

Again you see him
on his way to design the Thorndon pool
where your sister now swims in her bluegreen cap
a wave moving through the water.

Here he is studying the one
white shoe abandoned on the zig zag.
It's been there for weeks, the colour slowly
leaking into the concrete. A woman's shoe.
Next time you see him he's on his way to marry
your grandmother who has only one leg and on it
one white shoe.

*

Return home and Harry goes
outside, shutting the door
firmly behind him.

Drive to Lake Ferry and along the coast
to Cape Palliser.
Climb white steps high to the
lighthouse where your father works the
light as a young boy.

Back along the road to Ngawi and here's
Harry putting out to sea with his
brother—off to get the flour from
the store, off to lose it over
the side.

You wave and
wave they raise
a hand.

II. THESE DAYS

Estonian songs

The titles for these poems are taken from song titles on Veljo Tormis's recording Forgotten Peoples. *The recording is a set of six song cycles from the region of Estonia through Karelia and towards Finland.*

Waking the birds

Wake birds,
the sky loses its dark
because of you, light
slowly coming around
the corner to surprise
you.

A lion worries a bone
into morning
and berries come out
from behind their green
shields.

Boats in the harbour
planes in the sky
the wings and wheels of the
modern world are
moving.

Sang the mother, sang her daughter

Life is sad,
sang the mother
sang her daughter,
life is so sad,
because we can't read
and listen
at the same time.

The arrival of wedding guests

All night my friend tells me
she loves, she loves, she
loves her life.

She is my wedding guest
she arrives with her face
of happiness
and someone strikes up
a tune.

Instructing the newly-weds

Listen bride
listen groom
don't be afraid.
At night, the dark trees at the end
of the street—how frightening
they seem, then
morning comes and uncovers
nothing but leaves.

Praising the cook

They say the sexual impulse
is like a fiery horse.

When you break an egg
    one-handed
into the frying pan
it sounds like distant hooves
crossing a dusty plain.

When I, Chick, was growing up

I learnt many things
like   what happiness
can do.

When he said

this spoon's
for you

I felt so happy
and, years later,
so very sad.

A son or a daughter

On a night when the
moon moved solemnly
about the sky
a third daughter was born.
The unhappy doctor
went to the father.
I'm sorry, he said,
it's another girl.

Girls are good luck
said the father
If you don't have a daughter
you only know you're alive
because your shoes move.

My sister, my little cricket

Listen, sister,
sometimes it seems life's
not worth a bowl
of old onions
but, like travel,
you should stick with it
for the points of interest
along the way.

Take love for instance,
that's interesting
in any language.

My mouth was singing
My heart was worrying

O deceptive mouth
covering up
for the heart like that.

Urging her into the boat

I'll take some of that expensive brie
for Beverley, he said.

        Beverley? Beverley!
I cried, Quick, get into the
boat. O shy and beautiful
Beverley, bring your brie
and come with me.

Heavenly suitors

They come from the sky
with brandy snaps—like
kings.
Come with us, they
say. Weather won't
harm you.
Where we live
there is nothing
birds don't like doing
and everyone is
deciduous.

Suitors from the sea

They leave
the gay gordons
of the world
and cross the sea

home to me.

The oak cutter

Plant trees
in the top garden.

Not an oak—I'll
cut it down.

Plant blossom
so you can make
a swing.

What are they doing at your place?

What are they doing
at your place? The ballerinas
with their delicate
limbs, the startled
trees.
There was a good reason
but you've forgotten it
entirely. Now the man
with no hands
beckons them home.
The horses are out.
The tin cow loose
on the lawn.

The ox climbed a fir tree

The ox climbed a fir tree
to see what he could see.

He cried ah, my love
this view from above
is quite splendid,
you are smaller
than a dove.

He cried
ah, my love
I am enthralled
but now I can't see you
at all.

Ending and going home

Ending and going home
to where love
lives, high
above the town.

My favourite place,
where you find
sweet apples fallen
on the soft ground.

A weeping maiden

The world's in a
spin. Yellow continents turn
and turn until the
little caravan of feeling topples
forward and runs wildly
down the road.

Lullaby

Sleep gently little one
the world is a ball
it knocks quietly
against the window
in the wind
sleep gently
nothing will harm you.

Wedding song

Now you are married
try to love the world
as much as you love
each other. Greet it as your husband,
wife. Love it with all your
might as you sleep
breathing against its back.

Love the world, when, late at night,
you come home to find snails
stuck to the side of the house
like decoration.

Love your neighbours.
The red berries on their trampoline
their green wheelbarrow.

Love the man walking on
water, the man up a
mast. Love the light moving
across the *Island Princess*.

Love your grandmother when she tells you
her hair is three-quarters 'café au lait'.

Try to love the world, even when you discover
there is no such thing as *The Author*
any more.

Love the world, praise
god, even, when your aerobics instructor
is silent.

Try very hard to love
your mailman, even though he regularly
delivers you Benedicto Clemente's mail.

Love the weta you find on the path,
injured by alteration.

Love the tired men, the burnt
house, the handlebars of light
on the ceiling.

Love the man on the bus who says
it all amounts to a fishing rod
or a light bulb.

Love the world of the garden.
The keyhole of bright green grass
where the stubborn palm
used to be,

bees so drunk on ginger flowers
that they think the hose water
is rain   your hair tangled in
heartsease.   Love the way,
when you come inside,
insects find their way out
from the temporary rooms of
your clothes.

Red lorry yellow lorry

Late at night we lie in bed
and worry about
the children.

One has lucky ears.
The other, a thumb
like the buddha.

We don't want them
to grow up to be
the sort of people
a lake is always out
to get.

For Christmas we give
each of them a
wooden lorry—one
yellow, one red.

See what you can do with
the great sandpit of
childhood, we say.

Set up the roads and the
pit, the rough tracks
to take you places.

The journey

Where will you
want her to
be   this person
you'll call
family   and how
will you want her
to come to you?

Knowing she's welcome,
she'll make her way
from over
the plum coloured
sea, the long arch
of trees before the
high country, the
low country
the shy lake
the red singing
desert   all the
big stones arranged
to look like
animals
on the dark
plain earth.

The man Dean went to photograph

The man Dean went to photograph
has the Easter Island statues on
either side of his back, the
pyramids in between, across the
top the Pyrenees and above them
the sky. In between is a gap
he is worried about. He plans the
Niagara Falls down one
side, the pink and white terraces
down the other. He likes things
big so you can see them. Like
when he climbs the Pyrenees and
sees the country displayed
before him like the sea
inviting pleasure craft to play
upon its surface—he finds enormous
satisfaction in this. Likewise, when
he gazes down on the plain and
sees his wife, the great wings
of the eagle spread across her back
impatient to rise.

Weather

Air ripe
with the sea.
In the dawn, light
comes upon objects
in the same way that a
person newly returned
to a familiar place
touches things, with a sense
of remembrance, awe.

Later, in other rooms, but
rooms where light has also
visited, men and women meet
secretly, full of longing
and regret. And, later still,
all over the city people remember
the same dream, in which,
in another country, men on horseback,
and buffalo, and young
brides race for their
lives. They run at a terrible
speed. The animals' hooves
thundering, dust
rising, and the brides
striding out with such long
legs, their dresses slung up over
their arms as they run.

Travel

This is what happens.
You go out to the world
then return and want
to put your arms around
everything.

Spend the end of your
twenties on a boat between
islands, in the company of
mobile homes *Maui* and
Endeavour.

Climb into the freshly made
bed of the country.
Just before Timaru, *Phar Lap*
Motors, then *Timaru*
Windscreen and Glass Open
Forever.

Wanaka on a boat towards
snow. Get familiar with
the lake, the purple
hills. A plane rolls
in the lovely silver
light.

Turn thirty in Christchurch.
Your present a tea towel
Greetings from Opunake
both islands bright
green—you hold the
country in your
hands.

Tornado

For days we stayed
inside. Lit the lamps.
Some prayed.
Some made food.
The times the wind quietened
we told stories:
The time we loved a man so much
we thought we'd die;
the time our brother left
for war; the time we wondered
at our mother's sense
of purpose.
It was a difficult time.
All that frightening wind
and our lives
storming the house
like that.
When it finally stopped
we went outside
to view the
damage. The great
orchard of
our lives.
All those trees.
All that fruit.

Then Murray came

It was the morning for
selling the car, but
when I went out to start it,
it wouldn't go. Greg went
to get petrol on the bike. I
rang the A.A. Then Ray
arrived. I said *I'm sorry*, he
said *don't worry* and looked at
the car and at the wheels and
in the boot and said *she's a lovely*
old thing. He tapped the coil
and the fuel pump to try to
make it go. Greg came back
with petrol, but that didn't help.
Then, because there was nothing else
to do, we went inside and had coffee
and Ray smoked and talked about
going to Outward Bound and sleeping
and losing a stone.

Then Murray came.
He drove up the hill in his yellow
A.A. car, shaking his head. Got out and said
I was sure you were having me on. Last time I was
here you said you were selling it
and the other day I saw you walking
through town and I thought 'thank god she's
sold that thing'. He cleaned the carburettor
and laughed. Put more petrol in, replaced a
filter. I said *I wasn't joking, there's*
someone here who wants to buy it. Murray
laughed and said *sure. No, no,* I said, *it's*
true. Ray. See, there he is, up at the
window. Murray looked up and Greg and Ray
waved. *How much is he paying for it?* asked
Murray. I started to say and he stopped
me. Said *no, on second thoughts, don't tell*

me. I don't want to hear about this.
Ray came down and took over
holding up the bonnet of the car.
What's your name? he asked Murray.
Murray, said Murray. *Well I'm*
Ray, this is Greg and this is
Jen. Hello Murray, we said.
And then the car started.

Please, pay attention

(*after Carlos Drummond de Andrade*)

Please, pay attention.
The fig tree—it is in leaf,
with fruit, before you even
notice it is there.

Open your eyes.
Wind gusts
explode the sea's surface
in circles. The bad weather's
all gone to sea, they said,
but it's raining years
on your head, you'll
have to go inside and
close the door.

A boy on the bus carries
six sandwiches in plastic
wrap on his knees. Such
lack of inhibition! You could
learn from that.

Be wild and curious. The
day is in bloom. It needs
attention, admiration.
Bees graze the lavender.

There's a new yellow wall
sycamore trees come
over it.

from These days

It was a year of great sadness
in the garden. A sister
died. Our friends' wounded
marriage. A sick child. Another
sister died and they wrapped her
in cloth and we laid her
in the ground.   Rest
we hoped for. For the comfort
of a surface soft as paint
mixed with beeswax.
We hoped at least the animals
would remain, but
all the little dogs in the street
ran away from home—an Airedale
terrier called Lucy ending up
in a café in town.
Helpless in the face
of sick animals, we wept
over a hedgehog, held the hunched
body of our sleeping child
close. Solace came in small
ways—dealing kindly
with bees in the kitchen,
the sidestepping
of a moth across
a night window.
The child said here
I'll put my
arms around you
so you don't get lost.
After time a vase
entered our lives
as a body of light
its white flowers a kind of
peace we craved and
entered   as the gate
to another garden

on a hillside, tended by
women who looked up
from roses to mountains
and saw snow
bloom there.

❖

Days full
of taxi drivers.
One claims he's the longest-
serving driver in New
Zealand, another tells you
he spends his Fridays and
Saturdays thinking about
traffic and how
to avoid it. A third jokes
that he's so scared of heights
even shagpile carpet
makes him nervous.
You've had a good run.
The trips almost as interesting
as their destinations.
A bit like Cézanne
with his plain old
onions sprouting shoots
during the months it took him to
paint a still life.
You're pleased with the way
these things take on a life
of their own. Like that hair
of Basquiat's trapped
in his painting, one free end
in the air touring the world
while Basquiat goes
his own way, further into
earth, becomes
pigment—the colour of dirt
the colour of stone.

Martinborough

Drawn in by a rag
rug. Through the door to a
thirsty lawn done in by
summer   to the river
over burning stones   to the moon
a miracle that raises us
to our feet each
evening, leads us to the shed
where we sleep, the scent of
honey a light blanket we
lie under, listen to plums fall
on the dark floor of night.

Feel the doughnut

The child, too, names
everything, wants to take hold
of language, in the same way that
he tries to pick the pattern up
off the carpet.
We describe everything
find ourselves explaining
it's a tree
it's green and grows
in the ground.
There are leaves in the washing,
dominoes in the garden, a dream
adrift on the bathroom floor.
Sometimes there's a dog.
Worn out by narration, we let our hair
go—he looks like Jim Bolger, me
like Suzi Quatro.

Pears serious
on the table.
We eat ham sandwiches
made from leaves, there's jam
in the bed and milk
cool against your leg.
You turn on the radio and hear
It's really just a matter of
getting Jesus and the disciples
across the road.
If only it was that
simple. Instead you watch
men work on it—whole days
spent in the company of concrete mixers
and bulldozers,
their comings and goings punctuated
by men walking
for the good
of their hearts.
There's a man who knows
the wind speeds of storms,
gales and cyclones. Another
whose astronomer father
seduced him with pictures of
night skies lying around
the house. This son photographed
the sun as the moon, the afternoon
turning to evening before
his eyes.

Here there's a new moon
on the horizon—this landscape
he makes. Your heart and lungs
a lawn he might
play upon.
On the other side of the hill there's
Greta, newly born. A greeting
or sign of gratitude. Her black hair

lively punctuation,
her tiny wrists.

Wake to find another moon
still serene in the sky
just to the left
of the flagpole.
Hey, what's that big
marble up there?
It's fading quietly
over next door's shaggy
fig, over lavender,
over the child's morning hair
which resembles the sea
skiffled by wind, over our new
friends—knitted man and mr bunny,
over a semaphore of
pigeons in the valley and over
a sign inviting *come in, rest*
and pray   yes, yes, we say and
god bless the nesting
farm animals.

❖

Slow curl of
autumn
a fallen pear withers
caught in a vee of the
next-door tree
summer leaves
by the side door
moneymakers linger
on the edge of red
in the vegetable
garden.

Many monarchs
escape crèche

tour gardens
bordering this road wide
as a river, up which we
sail daily, belly
boisterous with child
and because this will be
the last time
you want to commit it
to memory, to paper,
record these upheavals—the
seasons' leisurely roll and
the push of an elbow or heel
a falling star traversing
the stretched sky.

❖

These days

These days, if we want
to talk to our brothers and
sisters, we go down
to the basement

Hello chairs, hello tables,
hello bookshelves, hello records
hello banana table, hello
printing press, hello rugs, hello
guillotine, hello other belongings
stored in boxes and suitcases.

Our brother sends books
from London, our sister
news of a river frozen
in Spain. From York, another
sister (who goes nowhere
without a roll of black masking tape
in her pocket) sends a transistor radio
wrapped in green felt

with instructions to lie it flat
and place the accompanying
tiny lighthouse on top.

The lighthouse stands
on its boxed ocean
of green, broadcasts
muted static into
our living room. It's the sound
of roiling sea. The sound
of distance. The sound of them
trying to reach us,
us trying to reach them.

❖

Up here, at the top
of the poem, we have
a pear, with leaves!
So much more *pear* than
those without. Further down
is the tree it might have come
from. One pear, caught
in a vee of branches, now
resembles nothing like
fruit, it has become an
other thing, dark wrinkle
collapsing in on itself.
Here is the rest
of the garden struggling
with summer's longevity
and us going about
in it—one of us round
with child, the child too
going about, over and
over inside you, inside
the garden. And here's
where you leave
the unweeded paths to see an

old friend become a priest.
Christ 'went about' and so
too will your friend who
knew you in the late surf
of childhood, and has
been gone for many
years. Now here he is
you've found him in this
poem, just at the point where
he kneels and the others draw near
and lay hands on his head
and on each other's arms
or shoulders and something passes
between them.

❖

In waiting

Here's winter coming up
the valley, the last
of the monarchs sailing
past the hillside's glossy pelt
of flax.

Farewell summer.
Farewell autumn.
We marvel at the seasons
and how persistent, through
all of them, the ivy
is, slowly dragging the washing
line earthwards. And how persistent
this child is, also heading
earthwards, yet turning back
again and again. Your body
too, persistent, longing for
memory to kick
into gear and relieve
this ache—dull—like

the soft thud of passionfruit
striking ground.

❖

He enters the world
slippery as his brother's sense
of geography.

You breathe him out
of your habitable body—little
seal, little pup,
tiny kid butting
at your neck.

His brother says *hello*
my little swiss roll
my little darling
my little doughnut

You welcome him into this
house, his new landscape
your voices his
memory—all he knew
before entering this din
of light.

❖

Coda
(*Carlo Victor Bornholdt*)

In Spain
your sister's bread lady says
with a name like that
that baby will be very successful
just like in a soap opera.

Villanelle

That summer that wouldn't go
the light was far too bright.
We didn't want to know.

But then we did. Slow,
or fast, the fight?
That summer that wouldn't go.

We couldn't know.
One thing we learned, though, was how might
fails, and that, we didn't want to know.

But then we wanted it all, blow
by crushing blow. After all, it was our right,
that summer that wouldn't go.

And so we sat it out. The glow
of light sinking into a night
we didn't want to know.

But it was the one sure thing. The only
thing we knew. And it was wrong, not right.
That summer that wouldn't go.
That summer we didn't want to know.

Pastoral

Spring we cleared the top garden.
Took it apart leaf
by leaf, stone
by stone; uncovered its
generous architecture till there was
not much left—taupata, rhododendron,
inconvenient old rose.
We worked, my mother, father and I,
while the children carted earth
about the lawn
in a small green
wheelbarrow.

Then summer began and
ended it all. We climbed down
the wide stone steps from the garden
and began to count.
From then we began
to remember him.

*

At his bedside
I read about figs
and mulberry trees
blackcurrants and
lemons. Tried to think
about the garden. About him
in the garden. Tried to memorise
his hands, his
whole lovely body
bent over the earth
as he dug.

To stop the weeds
I laid beds
of cardboard.
The garden became
a flattened box
and no one
ventured there.

*

We spent our days listening
to the engine
of his breath. His hands
questioned space
felt for branches
or new leaves
in the way our sons'
hands sought air out
when they were newborn.

We came and went
from his room—my mother
and sisters and I—making
tea, making small hopeless
noises, making trips across the road
for coffee, where we'd stand in line
behind the surgeon who'd held
our father's head
in his hands.

*

For days and nights we sat with him.
For all the days of his life we sat there
willing him to stay with us,
willing him to get up from the bed and
come away with us from there.
When it came time
of course he left us lonely.

We watched all night
and just as colour
leaked into the sky
all light left him
and day rolled up and
over us.

The jersey

A long time ago a friend
offered to knit me a jersey.
Because she was a busy person
we agreed she'd do it
when she found time.

A year went by and I moved away
from Dunedin (this was one of the reasons
for the jersey—it was very cold
and I didn't have enough
warm clothes).

I did buy a lot of second-hand coats
that year, and made do
with my father's old green fishing jersey
– one he'd been wearing the day he caught,
then lost, an enormous snapper
off the wharf at Golden Bay.

I was with him then
and remember the excitement
as we watched the fish
swirl up towards the surface
then the disbelief as the hook
came free and the great shape moved
away and down and down
until it became water
once more.

The jersey was a fine one
but rather large, as my father had been.
Fifteen years later the new jersey arrived
wrapped in brown paper and crammed into
our letterbox. It was a beautiful thing—
full of colour and texture. I am a tall person
but this jersey was made for someone much larger
than myself. Because of its size

and because I loved it but couldn't wear it
I put it in a cupboard while I thought
about what to do.

*

Then my father died and the world became a stopped
unsteady place.

After a time
I got back to doing the things
I'd done before.
Our son started swimming lessons.
In his class was a child named *Lyric*.
At the end of each lesson
she and my son floated
on their backs
while the instructor towed them
through the water.

There was a weird stillness about the children
when this happened.
It was as if someone had flicked
the sound off
carving a core of silence
into the pool's
noise and tumble.

*

I got the jersey out and decided to take it apart.
Because a lot of the wool was mohair and had been knitted
two strands together, it took a very long time.
It was complicated and frustrating and sometimes
I had to take to it with the scissors.
But even then I was grateful.

Please don't read too much into this.
I can imagine the temptation to see this jersey
as my life—here I was unravelling it (see,
already it's in balls in a bag on the floor)

ready to fashion into something else—
but it wasn't like that.

I don't mean to implicate my friend in this either.
She in no way set out to make anything
that would have to shoulder the responsibility
of metaphor. It was a jersey she knitted
and I am the one who took it apart.

Every evening I knitted peggy squares,
which were the simplest things
I could think of. And I would wear my father's
pyjamas—lovely striped cotton ones—
the kind of cotton that's so soft it feels
like silk. My mother bought him these pyjamas
to wear in the hospice
but he never even slipped his arm
into a sleeve.

*

After he died we gave away most of his clothes.
Other men in the family fitted his shirts.
His suits we gave to an organisation that helped
immigrant families. Some things we kept—
a man with one foot two sizes smaller
than the other, no one could ever step
into his shoes.

What do you do with cufflinks
all the little gold and silver bits
clinking in the dish?

His old green fishing jersey was long
gone. I'd never found it after I moved
from Dunedin.

It returned in a dream though.
A dream that came, I think, because of my friend
Mary, who found four boys' jerseys
in an op shop
in Milton.
She sent these jerseys to our youngest
son. Beautiful jerseys—striped and flecked
in colours you never see now
mostly because children
don't wear wool much
anymore.

We'd bemoaned this fact, Mary and I,
and that was when she recalled seeing the jerseys
and vowed to send them.
In the dream, my father's jersey—very old
and full of holes—was folded
beautifully but belonged
to someone else.
I couldn't bear to see it on their shelf.
Couldn't bear to leave it.
I woke, of course, and it
was gone.

*

It's the closest I've come to dreaming
about my father.
When he was ill, I woke one night
when he called my name
but even as I snapped
into consciousness I realised
he was on the other side of town
and I'd manufactured
his need for me.

*

Mary told me that as her mother
lay dying, she made sculptures from sticks
on the lawn outside her window.
All day this daughter
moved about the lawn
placing twigs carefully
on or against each other.

I wish I could have done this.

I wish I could have made something
in the face of my father's illness.
Instead, it became
a ragged hillside to be crossed,
furious with grief,
wondering at how unfaithful, how
ungrateful, his body seemed.

His illness
unmade me.
I wanted to climb back
inside the arms
of my first, strong, disintegrating
family. It made me fear
for my mother.
I didn't want
to let her out
of my sight.

*

Through that winter
after my father died
I knitted, and the pile
of peggy squares grew.
I took some pleasure
in laying them out
on the floor
to see how the colours
might go together.

*

For my forty-first birthday
I was given a tea towel
by my friend who had knitted
the jersey.
This tea towel features a
Horse Map of the World.
The horses stand proudly.
There's the *Connemara Pony*,
the *French Coach*, the *Shetland*
Pony, the *Mongolian* and *Polo*
Ponies, *Prejvalsky's Horse*, the
Darley Arabian, the *Clydesdale*
and the *Kentucky Saddle*, the
Mustang and the *Suffolk Punch*.

It occurs to me that
out of my knitting
I could make a horse
blanket. Not for one of these
Horses of the World
but for a horse my father rode
at Cape Palliser
in a photograph we have of him
as a young man.
My blanket would keep this horse
warm. It would love
it. The thought of this blanket
would mean this horse
would take my father out
over the roughest tracks
and always bring him
safely home.

Jack's shirt

I used to live in a road
that sounds like salamander.
Ferns grew in the letterbox.
I drove with my wrists.

The man who claimed
to love me then
then loved my friend, then
again, another.

That first friend had
a beautiful brother.
Still does. And the second?
It was her brother
I loved.

He wore school shirts
of a heavenly blue.
He gave me two. Then
left. They always do.
Or did, back then.

Back then they made
a cotton shirt that
lasted. Witness now
I have a shirt
that first brother wore.
I see him sitting, loose-
limbed, languid, in the
doorway, strumming a guitar.
Beside him stands the genius boy
who later died—made restless, pacing
in a garden.

I often wear this shirt my friend—
that brother's sister—gave me.
These summer days
I slip on my old, plain, cotton life
and go about in it.

The train to Nice

We could catch the nine twenty-three
or the ten seventeen, only the ten
seventeen doesn't go on Saturdays
or Sundays or holidays or on
the twenty-fourth of February. The nine twenty-three
runs every day. It's
circular. But no, not between
the twenty-eighth of February and the seventeenth
of May, or on holidays. Or
on the birthday of the driver and his
twin brother. Now that was a joyous
day, fifty-two years ago, just as the eleven twenty-eight pulled in
to the station. Les deux frères . . . ah . . . such cause
for celebration. Even Uncle Jean came down
from the mountains, leaving the dogs
and the goat, the olives and the hen.

Not Sundays either. Nor
Wednesdays. Nor between the hours of eleven
and one. Thursday though, that's the best day.
The train is fastest then.
That's the day the driver's mother makes
the bouillabaisse. That's the day the train
tears through the smaller stations.
That's the day she waves the spoon
in triumph. Here we come, here *he*
comes, racing down the tracks.

Train

The man at the corner
of the street says 'train'
and straight away I know
he's asking
where the station is.
Maybe he's going to see his
friend, or his sister. Or maybe
he's going to see about
a job. Or maybe it's his
father—his father who is dying
in the hospital.
Already he's walked
ten miles, having missed
the first train. He's eaten nothing
but some raisins he found
in his pocket, left there by his
child last time they went
to the beach.
So he's hungry and his feet
are aching and now he's here
at the tracks. He's been under the bridge
with the line going over
but he can't find the station.
It's like that dream he has
where he's trying to ring his father
on the telephone but keeps dialling
the wrong number.
Now here he is and here
are the tracks, but where
is the train?
There's a woman
coming up the road. She's carrying
a tiny paper cup with a spoon
balanced on top and this makes her look
as if she knows where she is going.
So he asks her. Rather,
he says the word 'train'

and she’s surprised, but she stops
and repeats it, ‘train’.
And then they both hear it
and she points and touches
his arm and he runs
oh how he runs.

Outings

Poor children—they're all tired
of the walking. The French

children, the Italian children,
the children of the Néo-

Zélandaise—they're all tired.
The feminine beach and the

masculine garden, the boy dogs
and the girl cars; they've been

past them all. They have
fatigue. They want to go home

to their motherly houses.
This little one, why, he has

so much hunger he doesn't
rain, he pours.

Saturday afternoon

It's warm and raining and
we're on our way home
after coffee and biscuits with
jammy middles, when we stop
in a dishevelled but happy state
outside *Claudio Coiffure.*
We've been considering
haircuts and while we're standing
talking, Claudio comes out and says
that we'd better come in,
all of us, so we do, and in no time we're seated
in a row—me and Felix and Greg—with
Claudio, Bruno and Sofia washing our hair.
Bruno asks about Felix, and when I say he has
a fringe, there's uproar—*impossible, a fringe*
in France—so Felix has the time
of his life, with spikes and gel and Bruno's
earrings, and I'm talking English to Claudio
because he says it's cheaper that way
and Sofia gets so carried away
that she washes Greg's hair twice.
Then the three of us have scalp massages
and Claudio says he'll make my hair
all *supple,* and as beautiful as his wife's, and Sofia,
she's drying Greg's hair and blowing air down
her front—all the way down to her beautiful, decorated
middle, and we're having such a good time
that we want them all to come and live
with us. But then we're finished and have
to go, so we say *ciao,* and Claudio gives Felix a
sports medal and we go out into the late
afternoon looking much better and a little more
Italian than when we went in. At home
we take photos of our new selves and Felix
hangs his medal on our bed head
and we go to sleep that night in our award-
winning bed and dream Italian dreams and what

our lives in that other country
might have been.

Being a poet

Yesterday I bought
a blender—blue—from
Briscoes, just like
Marion's. Today
we're dealing with the big
issues, like: *How the World
Began* and
*Can We Have Froot Loops
for Breakfast*?
Friends ask
what I'm reading.
By the bed is *Go, Dog. Go*.
We looked at it this morning
just before our fight
over the nature of
Weetbix. *But it's soggy
every morning*, I hear myself say,
*that's just what Weetbix does
that's just its way.*

Ode to the little hotel

Little Hotel
we love you
and in your little
rooftop room we love
each other, even though
we are big
and hardly worthy of such
a little bed.

*

We love the street
you stand on
which is neither long
nor short, but somewhere
in between. And we love
your neighbours
who are our friends—
smaller than us
and so ideally suited
to their address.

*

O Little Hotel we love
your breakfast room
your petit déjeuner
the crypt we reach by
steep narrow stairs
a bob and curtsy on the last
to miss the bottom
beam—we love
all this.

*

You are our first
and last of Paris, Little
Hotel. We love
your lightning and the
rinsing rain, the way
your white towels sound
the slap of surf
outside our room.

*

You are the rabbit
of Paris. The duck
with beans and peas.
Little Hotel you are
our herb and cheese,
our soup and sauce,
you are all of these.

*

O Little Hotel
we love your lift
in which we are
always pleased
to know each
other, pressed so close
as we are.
And when we take them
we love your stairs—
wide enough for one
winding up to light.

*

Little Hotel
your windows through which
we duck and climb
to stand on your roof
and look out over
other roofs, we hold these
dear to us.

*

You are paint and wood
and stone and all things made
from these. O Little Hotel
you are a gallery
of leaves.

*

You are our pink suit
of Paris, Little Hotel, our men
in shorts, our jazz band.
Later we will slap our knees
and remember you as four musicians
outside the Sorbonne.

*

O Little Hotel
in whose room
we read and
rest a little
after long days
we revere you.

*

O Little Hotel
we will never
forget you. We will write
and we will return.
O Little Hotel
doorway to our city
of Paris
au revoir.

Peach, the jam

Ladder against a plum tree is code
for jam. There's rhubarb
too, and New Zealand spinach in
a French vegetable garden—
they're eating our greens here.
We're in the middle of nature—
it's *truly* rural, as our youngest
says, i.e. I can truly fly, that is truly
a dog. And there are kittens
who find a moving pen more fun
than leaves.

Sitting by the stream I keep
half an eye out for the large green
snake which passed by
the other morning. Are snakes
creatures of habit? Do they bite
writers? Storm warnings for Europe
and we have just put the washing
on—isn't that always
the way.

When the weather strikes we think of
the clifftop castles—great stone arks
riding the storm
like Roethke's glasshouse.
Down here it's all noise. We can't tell
if it's the wind in the trees
or the stream, the water
or the leaves. No matter. What blows in
is a fearful dream—waking, I realise
it was a Harry Potter dream—see, books can
affect your life. My sister said a black dog
(read *death*) would come for me, then my
father appeared and tried to make everything
all right. This is one of the few dreams I've had

about my father. The thing that still
shocks me about his death
is that he is so gone from us.
So truly gone.

Morning after the storm we open
our broody hen door and drive
through the Gorges des Galamus—
recent home to an hospitable
hermetic nun, her house built into
rock. Now you can buy a cup of tea
or an ice cream from outside the door.
Head for the Abbey and jam-making
monks. We buy confiture de pêche,
drive home along roads marked
je t'aime in huge white letters,
like a sign. We follow it.

Blue shirts, descending

(*after Apollinaire*)

I was happy
in the South,
so happy with what
I smelt and saw—
wild mint near the washing,
peppery roquette on opening
the door.
It was so good
that the moon
hung around for much
of the day, anxious not to miss
anything. And the light . . .
the light on her blue shirt,
descending . . . the
lights . . . even the fig tree shone
at night.
All transport lived
in a suitcase
and the children travelled
in search of the past
at the speed of two
horses, but carefully,
so as not to break
the eggs.
So happy were we
at our friends' house
that I emptied my
pockets, then emptied them
some more, then
surrendered my pockets
to the wall.
Three quiet skirts
circled over all.

Helen's house

(for Helen Cooper)

Summer's over
when the bath
comes back inside,
when a painter moves into
the gatehouse, up stairs
which rise over
a bicycle, overgrown,
memorial to its
ninety-two-year-old
rider.
Four strong men
return the bath
to its room where
eight young women
slept. Upstairs,
through a trapdoor,
one's mother rests
in a bedroom
which was once
the kitchen. The kitchen
now where the entrance
was, bathroom neat
in a cupboard, bed
where the shower used to be.
The inventive architecture
of mothers and
daughters. Days
are shorter now.

Confessional

Saturday afternoon walking along the waterfront
thinking about a haircut and how I might

call into Claudio's and that set me wondering
about why I waste time *thinking*

about having my hair cut, why don't I just do it? I don't
even like my hair. My first boyfriend used to

jokingly compliment me on its *mouse-brown-*
ness as we lay kissing and listening to music

on his parents' living-room floor. I never had
much luck with boys. I was also thinking about

personal poetry and how it's not given much
time of day any more, and how

when people talk about poetry
they often mention *compression*—yes, it can

be that, but it can also be a great sprawling
thing. And Kenneth Koch has died.

*

A good example of wasting time thinking about
trivial things: I was walking home

after a morning spent revising this poem
and stopped to look at some trousers being sold

at the side of the street by an African man.
The fabric was lovely and I asked how much

he wanted for them. *How much do you want to pay?*
he asked. *I don't know*, I said, *I'll have to think*

about them. Why do you have to think about them?
he said, *why can't you just think about them now?*

Yes, she who hesitates is lost. Another thing
is that I always feel more comfortable in other people's

clothes. My friend Sarah's cast-offs are the most
favoured items in my wardrobe. As someone who is

not very adept at shopping I should probably pay Sarah
to buy clothes she likes, but in her heart-of-hearts

knows she won't wear, then she could just pass
them on.

*

I'd like to mention my children. I hope they know
that I love them even though I yell sometimes.

At the eldest because he continues to leave his
wet towel in a heap on the floor, despite my saying

many times *it won't dry there*. Every time I say
these words I feel like somebody's mother and then I realise

I *am* somebody's mother—three people's in fact—
and a lot of time is spent cajoling them into eating

breakfast and making star charts and when I'm not losing
my temper I try my best to be *positive* and *encouraging*.

And I wonder *how did this happen?* Sometimes I find it hard
to make the jump between *then* and *now*.

*

Now is the Katherine Mansfield room in Menton, France.
In the time I have been here orange blossom has flowered

and gone, next-door's kiwifruit has taken a firm hold
on the fence and their avocado is a shambles of new leaves.

A passionfruit vine has come over the wire, flowered and is now
laden with fruit. It's been a fecund old time.

*

When I started work here I spent a lot of time
watching the crane driver on the building site which

backs on to the railway line which runs in front of
this room—yes it's noisy sometimes, but I've become

used to it. I wanted to see the driver leave his cab
and climb down the crane. During this time a friend

in Wellington met and kissed a crane driver
at a party. It's odd the way these things coincide.

I didn't want to kiss this crane driver, I merely wanted
to see him climb down. For days I watched and always

missed him. I'd sit for ages, go inside to drink some water
and come back to find him gone. One day I sat all morning.

I saw him lean forward to yell out the window to the men
below (I loved that—all this technology and the crane driver

still opens the window and hollers). I saw him reach back—
water maybe, or food. I saw the crane work way past

the dinner hour and it grew so hot on the doorstep where
I sat that I had to get my hat. Just a few seconds and he

was up and out of that cab. I caught him as he jumped
lightly on to the platform then watched as he came down,

hand over hand down the metal ladder. I went inside.

*

Reading over that part of the poem, sitting in the ancient
green deckchair outside the writing room in the shade

of the earlyish morning, I look up and down he comes
again, as if summoned (*hey, how about that*, I would say

if I were American). About ten rungs down, he stops
and I imagine takes in the view of the soft, still

Mediterranean—one of the boys said this morning *It looks
like you could get a white crayon and draw all over it*—

then he reached for the red T-shirt slung over his shoulders
and it fell, down through the circle of the ladder like . . .

like what? Like a red T-shirt falling down the inside
of a crane. Someone on the ground is whistling.

*

When I saw the X-rays of my father's cancer—all of us
with him in the room while the surgeon pointed to the dark

smudges that meant maybe three or four more months
of life—I tried to think what those marks looked like,

whether they resembled anything, but no, they remained
what they were—dark patches marring a lit screen, changing
everything.

*

On Saturday (the one we started with) I was walking home
along the waterfront noticing the young women and their beautiful

skin and the way their bodies are so firm and lovely
and I remembered that we used to look like that

though I never gave it much thought at the time. It wasn't until
age started that I realised I too would wrinkle and fold and

mark and that everything would settle down and sure enough
it did. I don't actually care too much about this (I think because

I associate that youthful time with fragility and unhappiness). Now,
I'm prepared to trade 'beauty' for a body that's strong and useful—

Polyanna, I can hear my friend Marion cry. At the beach
it's the elderly I really want to look at. Alone, almost

naked, they give themselves up to the sun, as though it's the source
of all they need to continue on in the world. Always

the men lie on their sides, scant hair rimed with salt,
long thin arms across sunken boned chests. *Ratcheted*

seems the word to describe these arms, but
it's not correct. Flesh sags and settles against stones.

The women rub their bodies absent-mindedly the way they might
brush crumbs from a tablecloth. As the sun cools, children dig

by the water, parents read, and the elderly relax and slow,
sleep settling over them like a thin sheet. Down they go,

hand over hand through the bright of their lives. We swim
and talk and bucket and build and rub and brush and scoop

and watch and tousle and chide, while the elderly, skin crumpling
into skin, they climb on down.

III. PEARLY EVERLASTING

Summer

New white sheets
on the line.
Even the pegs
are warm.

Our youngest son
leaks sand.

Iris the dog snores
on the green sofa.

Cat!

Out!   we cry.
My husband glows
in the dark.

Concert

New leaves
on the old rose.
White blossom
on the black doris
plum.
You go out
from your name
to life's
haberdashery, sit next
to a photographer
with surfer's ear
at a concert by the
consort, in the carillon.
There's the woman
with the interesting waist
and so much sound
inside her body
that water leaks
from our eyes;
and the conductor, we are also
moved by him—his affirming
mouth, fingers wriggling
like bait.

Not go away

(*Waihi Beach, February* 2005)

Pitched tent.

The baby with the
crinkled ear
creaks
in her pram.

Our father's ashes
nourish
the macadamia tree.

Broken up by sunlight
a boy turns over
a year
and the wind blows out
the candles.

Cheese is my life declares
one brother. *I think girls*
*are **fond** of shy boys*
but that's as far
as it goes, says the other.

At dinner time
we find the missing piece
of our one-thousand-piece jigsaw
in the fridge.

There's no salt left
in the duck.

Women and men

Louise Cake—recipe contributed
by Louise—it's in the oven.
I'm in the shade of the washing, reading
A Pair of Scissors by Sharon Thesen and
the phone goes and I don't answer it
even though it might be the plumber,
Pete, or the builder, Steve.
Then the oven timer goes and I put a white stone
on the page—don't go away Sharon
I'll be right back
after checking on Louise.

Flannel

Flannels—how useful
they've become
with the bikes.
Knees, elbows, hands
and for the forehead
to calm the dishevelment
of fever.
Each child in its bed,
the mother—hardly
a flâneur—runs
between the two.
She remembers
a conversation overheard:
Just remember,
if you need me
I'll be gone.

Medical

She listens
to your chest
with such
concentration . . .

There's all the loud
machinery of course
and June—do you mean the month
or her name?
Her name is inside you
and audible, and the dream, too,
in which you try to fax your publisher
a cake.

She hears us remember
the cats and their soft fur
birds going ape
in the trees.

She can hear
the domestic
rattle around
like small change—
cake call
from the oven,
sigh of the tired
pots and pans, rice
slip into water
like a swimmer.

She hears
your upset.
The watermelon bought
to cheer you up
from a place with an aisle
marked 'instant dissolve food and drink'.

Erratic door,
a lack of iron,
the fence
creaking in the wind
like your knees.
Everything hurts
if you *hitch a hip*
says the physio
as her fingers wade
the river of muscle
which runs the bank
of your spine.

She hears your watch cough
politely, bellow of weather
appease the garden's thirst.
Lone plum on the tree,
long soft body of the stick insect
traverse the rampant rose.
She hears the love you have
for your husband.

Hears you kiss the baby
then drive across town
in your pyjamas
in the early morning, past
planes in a queue
on the runway. The man who
leans across *here, have a chocolate*
person.

Anger rise
like steam
off hot asphalt
on the runway.

Your friend, her dodgy
neck, her low
morale.

Listening, she can hear
the spades as they dig down
for the elderly beloved
cats. She hears children and adults
weep, 'all things bright and
beautiful' sung
over the graves, then the car doors
close as we head
for the beach.

A week of sun, then
the weather moves on.
We don wetsuits
the dinghy rocks
on the porch
tree saws
on the roof
the baby says
no no no no
and refuses to get
to her feet.

All night
insects flip and click
while the wind roars

suck and blow
suck and blow

and the curtains rattle
on their tracks.

A long way from home

I was a long way
from home. White bed

in the A&E Department. Someone saying
I'll get the morphine

from the trauma trolley. Someone else
A cup of tea? I am visited by an African

orthopaedic specialist—male—with the unlikely
but appropriate name of *Joy*. In London

my sister has her groceries checked at the supermarket
by a young woman named *Comfort*.

I lie still, remember the child who said:
It's like those times when you wake

then slide into thinking. Yes. I slide and remember
reading. How, as a child, books were the lens

through which I eyed the muddy track to adulthood.
I read for language and the way the words gathered

to make story. I read to understand and not
understand.

*

For six weeks now I've been outside of weather
and of reading. Outside of myself.

Pain taking up all the air in the room. In the
hospital ward my son, Jack, brings his art history essay

to visit. In it he's quoted from a book, *German Romantic
Painting* by Michael Vaughan. In his bibliography,

Michael is circled and the lecturer has written above:
William? Jack laughs, and as I am, and always have been,

a long way from the oval, explains: Michael Vaughan is
the captain of the English cricket team.

*

Mrs Buchanan's hearing aid is lost in the bed.
the nurse needs it so it can be charged. For tomorrow.

What's happening tomorrow? asks Mrs Buchanan.
Why, it's another day, replies the nurse. Over

the intercom: *I need a couple of nurses in room nine*
for a roll.

*

I have tried to read, but nothing
sticks. That anchor of my life has been raised and

I'm all at sea. I realise how much of myself I define
by reading. Someone once said they didn't think I was a

driven person. They meant as a writer, and I was hurt
by this. Realising, I think, that they were correct.

I would always describe myself as a driven reader,
though. Something very large is missing

from my life. While in hospital, I read an entire issue
of a New Zealand literary journal. Many of my friends

are in it. The main piece is one friend,
a novelist, interviewing another—again, a novelist

—who is dying. There are poems and prose
pieces by other friends. I feel safe in the company

of these friends who are also writers. Even
seeing their names on the contents page

is comforting. I read this magazine from cover
to cover and felt involved and

satisfied. When I returned home a week later
I picked the magazine up and had no memory

of the writing inside it, although I remembered
the feeling of reading each page. The contents

I miss. Reading has become the child at the end
of the bed, willing me to wake. The soup I couldn't

spoon, the food I couldn't take. It has become the
glass of water I reach for in the night,

the bell . . . the light.

December

We're all an uncle
down now
and hasn't the garden
gone mad—convolvulus
up to the top of the plum,
weeds rampant through
the rose.

You've spent too much time
in the hospital
with its lines and lures,
elbows grazed on the sheets,
someone always calling out
for *air*   or   *Ian*

long to be home
in the everyday wreckage
of the kitchen, to wake
next to your husband,
dusty with sleep,
light shining
through his ears.

Life

This new
quiet life.

At the end
of the day—

three lines
a cake
Peggy's son's
peas, Jane's damson
jam.

Mrs Winter's jump

We're coming out
from under
dismal. The sun is up
and so are the children,
mucking about
with skateboards.
He's out the back
playing 'Mrs Winter's
Jump'. And jump
she does. She
gathers up
her rusty skirts
and crosses all the
crooked space
between us.

Fitter turner

It was a year when our bodies
surrendered—knees, backs, lungs—listen

to your shoulder, instructed my physiotherapist,
who was also studying English Literature

at university. *Wild nights/ Wild nights* she'd quote
from Emily Dickinson as she massaged my neck

which is still sometimes sore after one parachute jump
too many, twenty years ago. Risk was what I thought

was needed, and yes, risk was good, but I had
a tendency to overdo it. What wrecked

my neck this time was the garden. It also
took a toll on his lungs, which do not suffer pollen

gladly. The family cold, which hung around
for five weeks, showed no sign of departing,

on top of which I lost my voice, which caused
confusion at the doctors when I went after being

bitten by something in the garden. My arm
started to swell and the inflammation crept down

towards my elbow as I struggled to explain that it
wasn't my lack of voice I had come about.

Pulling my sleeve up seemed to work and the doctor
was very impressed, as was the medical student

who accompanied him. The doctor drew around the swelling—
a shape that by this time resembled a very large and interesting

potato—and said that if it got much bigger, or if I began to feel
unwell, I should come back up smartly. That night

the temperature plummeted. There was thunder
and lightning and hailstones the size of marbles.

We stayed inside for the next two days, with everybody
coughing and me unable to speak, resting my sore, red arm

while the new ceiling insulation watched over us.
At this point I remember someone commenting on

an earlier poem of mine, which resembles this one,
saying some people might think *it's not poetry*. Well . . .

There were the colds and the neck and the lungs and
the bite and then there was the hip, which is

connected to the knee, though not literally.
In between is the femur which my friend Marion

has broken. I have a Dutch hachee in the oven (for the purposes
of this poem—if in fact it *is* a poem—I will call it

a *casserole*), which involves lemons and cloves and which
I have made twice successfully, once unsuccessfully,

before. (Currently I am going through a phase where nothing
I make tastes of anything. Or, everything I make

tastes of nothing. I hope the casserole doesn't fall into
this culinary hole.) Shortly after the neck came the knee,

which is where this poem really began. To explain . . .
something happened which made me want to add

to a poem I had thought was finished. I tried,
but I had been right in the first place—that poem had

somehow closed its doors, in the way poems do,
so I had to begin something new.

*

My knee I injured running up stairs at the National Library.
I knew this was not a good idea, but I was at work

on a poetry exhibition, excited, and full of a great sense
of urgency (poetry can do this to you). All day I ran

up and down the stairs in search of books and manuscripts.
When I woke the next morning my knee was sore

and I couldn't bend it very easily. I felt
an impending sense of doom. Since I was quite young

I have had *bad knees*—the right always worse
than the left. At 14, I had six weeks of plaster, then

an operation, then another six weeks of plaster, after which
my leg emerged, wasted and looking and feeling as if

it belonged to someone else. Around my knee
was an impressive scar shaped like a question

mark. After a lot of physio and lifting weights
made from my father's socks filled with sand

and draped over my ankle, my knee improved. It's years ago
now, and although it still troubles me sometimes, mostly

it's all right. I'm not meant to run or play sports—like tennis
or squash—which involve sudden changes of direction.

Poetry, being low impact, is fine. After the stairs,
I went to see the orthopaedic specialist who carved

the question mark on my knee. For the purposes of this poem
we'll call him *Chris*. (We might as well, because that's his name.)

We talked about joints and their weaknesses and that led us
to my father's rare, wonky ankle, which Chris told me

had been written about in a *British Medical Journal*. He promised
to find the article in the medical library and send it to me.

*

After my knee recovered and the poetry exhibition
opened, I began writing in my shed, which is up on the lawn

at the back of our house. Am I working hard? Yes, I am.
I've been writing and thinking and clearing a space

near the vegetable garden for another shed. This time
for the children. It's been good working to make room

for this shed, even though it's meant some mornings spent
with the shovel, instead of working on this poem. I've developed

a sore back, but nothing serious, just an ache. Like my sister
who wrote from London to say, among other things,

that she'd hurt hers again getting off her bike.
We're all getting older and sadder.

*

Clearing a space for the shed has meant packing
the vegetable garden into cardboard boxes and

moving it down the steps to outside the kitchen
door. Once the shed is built it can go back again

but I'm fearful of plants being trampled.
Shaun—our builder—is careful, but he thinks a lot

about surfing and sometimes doesn't watch
where he's putting his feet. Occasionally

he doesn't turn up, because the southerly has dropped
and the surf is good. I don't mind this. I like the fact

that he also has his mind on other things.
I knew he was all right when he walked past

the kitchen door one day and said *I smell soup—*
have you got a bacon hock in that?

*

Fitter turner is an occupation I've been thinking about
lately. The words doing just that in my head. It's because of

my father's ankle. I think he could've done with someone
in that trade. Every day these words come to me, and then,

in the mail, comes the copy of the article about my father's
ankle, written when I was two. It's entitled

Congenital ball and socket ankle joint and talks of
a boy, aged five—my father—being admitted to hospital

with a disease of the cervical spine. This article recounts
how, later, my father, aged 21, presented with:

> *a fracture of the tip*
> *of the lateral malleolus*
> *of the right ankle.*
> *A small effusion was present*
> *in the joint. A ball-and-socket*
> *ankle joint was present,*
> *and both tibia and fibula helped*
> *to form the proximal articular*
> *surface. The scaphoid was fused*
> *to the talus and the cuboid*
> *articulated with the 4th*
> *metatarsal. The 5th metatarsal*
> *was absent. Only two cuneiforms*

were present. The second toe
had only two phalanges.
The right limb was almost
1 inch shorter than the left . . .
No abnormality was noted
in the skull, chest, abdomen,
pelvis, hands, knees
and renal tract.

That came later.

The X-rays of my father's spine, ankle and foot
were the saddest things imaginable. I went outside

and moved some earth. For two days I did this,
until my back ached and my knees hurt so much

I couldn't do it any longer. I went back
to my shed and looked at the pictures again.

For an odd moment I imagined those bones of my father's
in the ground. But we didn't bury him. He burned

and became ash. When the red curtains in the crematorium
shushed closed to conceal his coffin, our son called out

hey!—startled by the trick of it all.   *Hey!*   it was what
we all wanted to say. The ash my father became

was shocking in its greyness and grittiness.
We scooped handfuls and scattered what he now was

on the ground. What more can you say about this?
Hey!

That it is not the worst thing that can happen?

*

In the middle of writing this poem I had a dream
I was wrestling with the ghost of Katherine

Mansfield. A friend suggested it was a poem
I was struggling with. Yes. *This one.* Which I know

seems very plain and straightforward and
conversational, but it's taken a lot to get it

this way. Today I will take the casserole to Marion
who can now manage on one crutch, which is good,

because her husband (who coached the rowing crew
I was coxswain for, after being told I shouldn't row

on account of my knees) is about to have a knee
replacement and she needs to be able to get around.

Tomorrow I fly to Nelson. I don't like flying,
but I will grit my teeth and get on the plane.

Last time I flew on a small plane,
the pilot said before take-off *Lifejackets*

are under your seats. If anything happens, put them
on. Don't wait for me to tell you what to do

because I'll be out of here. In Nelson I will be met
by a woman who describes herself as having

'the ponytail of indifference'. I look forward
to this. She will drive me to the Rosy Glow

Chocolate Shop, above which I will stay. I will
lie down on the comfortable bed, then I will

get up and go and read some poems. Later
I will go to a Haydn Mass with the woman

with the ponytail, who will sleep a beautiful,
attentive sleep through the third and fourth movements.

Next morning I will buy some chocolates from
Rosy Glow and go to the airport in a taxi driven by

'Dickie', who has woken up deaf in one ear.
Maybe the doctor? I will yell. *Twelve thirty*

he'll reply, then pass me a mint. I'll head home
on a plane flown by a pilot who doesn't know

his left from his right, and from the air I'll see
our house and my shed and the frame

of the new shed taking shape by the vegetable garden.
The weather will be beautiful and I'll remember

that today is the day a friend may learn that his life
will be shorter than he would ever wish. Two friends

will tell me their mothers are dying. My son
will collect a cricket bat in the face and his eye

will turn the colours of evening. To pass the time
at the hospital he will ask me to list the things

that never end: space, time, the universe,
dogs barking at the mailman, numbers, weather,

fear, love, kindness, television, Haydn's mass . . .
Then a doctor will come, and because we live

in a very small pocket in the great big frock
of the world, he will be the chairman of my son's

school board of trustees. He is a kind man and a good
doctor, and he will patch up my son's cheek and we'll

head home. On the way I will think about the poetry
reading and how, beforehand, I met a man who makes

furniture, but originally trained as a fitter and
turner. *Do I know what that is?* And how,

in the middle of the reading, I glanced down at my book
and a tiny green preying mantis

scrambled bright and awkward over the page.
I will tell my son about this. He will suggest

I might have carried the insect in my bag, all the way
from Wellington, all the way from the vegetable garden

in boxes, and I'll say *yes, I might have.* And we'll agree
that wherever it came from, it seems like a good sign.

And we'll drive home—his eye matching sky—which is
an easy rhyme, but pleasing, to me, nevertheless.

Big minty nose

Coming up out of pain, coming up out of
nothing but body, to find the world

is full of weather and has a *big minty nose.*
Stick insects ride the dog rose

the garden trembles
with birds.

*

Huge winds have brought down the climbing rose
behind my shed. I struggle for a long time to try

to raise it, but its weight defeats me. I move close—
leaves in my face, thorns in my hands—then away

and the scent of mint rises from where my foot
has grazed the herb growing by the path. Pain,

pleasure, pleasure, pain. That seems to be
how it goes. In the end I prop the rose up with the hoe,

then a ladder, and try climbing out the window
to haul it up from there, but there's nothing

to hold on to and I'm taken by how absurd
this all is—the window unable to open properly

because of the rose, me too big to fit easily
through the window, the rose too heavy . . .

in the end I rig up a pulley system with nails
banged into the shed and some rope and I slowly raise

then secure the lot to an old dangerous piece of metal
that sticks out of our lawn. Some years ago my father

stuck a tennis ball on top of it to stop people breaking
their ankles. I leave the rose because I need to think about it

and head down the steps for a needle
to dig the thorns out of my hands.

Does this make me part rose?

*

After a year of illness, I began to walk again.
At first, still on crutches, just a short distance

down the road. Then around the block. Then
I ventured further. And further. It was like reclaiming

the world. I greeted everyone I saw along the way
because I felt so pleased to see them, so pleased

to be upright and moving. I felt so pleased with the
days and the air and I felt so pleased to see

even the surly older man whom I passed every morning for
months and who has, only now, begun to smile.

*

Walking around the waterfront some mornings in winter
the wind was so strong I could barely move.

At times I was scared I'd be blown into the sea
or on to the road. Runners would approach,

hurled towards me, and we'd laugh, in the brief moment
in which they passed; me grounded, them in flight.

These days, while walking, I think a lot about compost.
Mixing up, breaking down, renewal—all the big themes.

It's a bit like baking, or making bread. I've been doing
a lot of that lately. My friend Susanna has given me some of her

sourdough bug, and our bench is the scene of much
mixing and rising. This bug I divided and passed on to

Trish when we met in town for lunch. She handed over *her*
sourdough bug, which is quite different in consistency

and needs a different rise. Susanna's bug came from friends
who moved to Singapore, and it now resides

in a number of households around Wellington.
Bread in our house is known by name—

Susanna's or Trish's. *Whose bread is it?*
the children ask when they see me adding flour

to the bowl. This bread is eaten with Jane's
damson jam, Chris and Margaret's honey, or

school marmalade; often in the company of
Marion's catmint, Nettie's daisy, the builder's rose.

*

Planting flax in front of my shed I raise large, sodden plugs
of earth, place flax in the holes, then stomp the earth back

in the same way that my father used to in our garden when
I was growing up. I can see his boots on the earth

and the brown skin of his calf muscle tighten as he trod
the soil down around the new plants. Sometimes I think

I am becoming my father. I buy blood and bone because
he used to. *What's blood and bone?* asks our youngest.

It's just that—blood and bone, but ground up.
Blood and bone! That's disgusting.

I rarely dream about my father, but sometimes
I'm startled because I think I see him in town.

I can't bear airports. All those men in suits.
Sometimes the sight of a shirt cuff below the arm

of a suit jacket can send me back years.

*

I have just cut the big fallen branch of the rose,
dragged it down the steps and across the road

to where men are pruning and mulching
our neighbours' trees. All the way down the steps

and along the path, the rose snagged,
reluctant to leave the garden. Now I'll fix

the remaining branches to the shed,
maybe buy some sort of canvas sling for support.

*

Yesterday, in a shop in town, I watched two young women fuss
over a display. What bothered them was the angle

of a grey shoe beside a handbag. I felt enraged by this
because milk is now more expensive to buy

than Coca Cola, and soon there will be no doctors
in the children's cancer ward at Wellington Hospital.

Placement of a shoe seemed to be the last thing anyone
in this country should be worried about.

This morning I learned that another father
of three has cancer. I planted an apple tree by the shed

—nobody's apple, just an apple—with more of Margaret's
blue daisy underneath for company.

*

When I was ill, time slowed and stopped, except
in the laundry, where a child's watch beeped

on the hour and the Harry Potter clock
ticked its way through the year. In hospital

I slept next to a woman on an air mattress named
Nimbus 3. When pain happened I would think

sometime this will be the past.
And now it is.

*

Days hurtle by with all the weight of memory
behind them.

*

I've been thinking a lot about our friend, Nigel,
who died. He and I shared a time of

illness. His much graver than mine.
It seems wrong to write of them in the same

sentence, or even the same poem, but this is not
about comparison, it is simply the way

it was. One late summer afternoon
we went to the beach. Nigel frail

in his pyjamas, me on crutches, others
with cushions and Greg with a dinghy

on his back. We sat and watched
as the children rowed back and forth

across the bay and a seal rolled lazily
nearby. It was a perfect day. All we wanted

was to row our friend away
from suffering.

*

Often when I'm up in the shed working on
this poem, I get drawn out into the garden.

I'm typing this with muddy hands, after stopping
on the way here to pull some weeds. Yesterday

I began work then found myself out
behind the shed where the rose grows,

wondering how to make a raised bed. I think the garden
is as much poem as this poem is. And the washing and the coffee

are also poem. The men next door with hammers and
saws, they have become poem, along with

the steps and the stick insects—one red, one green—
stuck to the shed window, looking in.

Maxim and Costa, the young boys I see
on my walk each morning—always trailing

something interesting to school—they have become
poem. And the men burning bees out of a flax

bush, they also have become poem. The seeds
on my sleeve and the spider scrabbling

on the desk, blown in from somewhere,
all are poem.

*

Because Nigel and I grew up in the same small
city and because we attended the same secondary

school, though not together, I felt we knew each other
in a way that didn't come through conversation

or meeting. He sold books in a shop I discovered
when I began venturing into the proper 'town'.

When I had my first poems published, he
stopped me at the counter and we talked,

for the first time, about books.
I will always remember that time,

his kindness.

*

Today while the pasta sauce was cooking
I iced a chocolate cake, dried the dishes and vacuumed

half the living room. Put coffee on, hung out the washing
and put a second load on. Our son Jack rang

from Auckland, laughed, told me he didn't go
to the *boobs on bikes* parade because he had to attend

an ethics lecture. I made afghans and remembered
I had to remember a dental appointment. Sometimes,

to make my life more interesting, I empty the dishwasher
in the afternoon, instead of the morning.

*

Things to do: Put the 'i' back in 'Clare'; dismantle
the table of war.

*

I go to the funeral of the mother of our childhood
friends. Her eldest child, now 60, stands to speak:

I am the first son, he says, and here we are—all
the sons and daughters. My father was father

to three daughters: the first daughter, the
second daughter and the third. The eldest,
the youngest, and the middle one. When he

was dying he asked me if I'd called
a taxi. He obviously had a destination

in mind. Never one for public transport, he was
keen to make sure he arrived on time.

*

Halfway to 94 and here I am with the oven cloth
in the garden. I ran down the steps

in the middle of planting a hebe
(Raewyn), because I remembered the bread

(Susanna) in the oven. When I got back
to the garden I found I still had the cloth

in one hand, trowel in the other.

*

It's so quiet you can hear the washing dry.

*

Days get away on us. And where do they go?
They go to the neighbours', where Karen is pruning

the pear tree. Our cherry tree (I first typed *cheery tree*)
used to shade Karen's house, and broke the fence. *That tree*

will always want to be a bigger tree said the arborist.
In the same way that the houses in our street

want to be bigger houses, and this poem will always want
to be a bigger poem.

*

What I wonder about is how much you need
to know? What if I don't have a garden?

What if I do still have a father?

*

In an earlier poem, full of grief
about my father, I wrote about my friend, Mary,

who made sculptures out of tree branches on the lawn
for her mother, who lay dying.

A few nights ago we launched a book by Nigel,
our friend who died, and for two days

I've been back inside the time of my father's
death. I was thinking about my friend and her

construction and then a message came
that she had begun to make

another of those stick works—twenty years
after her mother's death. She's been gathering

branches and standing them against the side
of the house, walking around, looking at them.

In the same way that I stand around and look
at this poem, work around it in the garden.

*

I'm not sure if the new apple tree will survive
the gales. The fence my son and I built

around the vegetable garden is, amazingly,
still upright. We made this fence after I got a quote

which contained far too many numbers, so we
drove to Placemakers and bought sturdy wooden

stakes and they gave us some wooden pallets, free,
from the timber yard. They are very good at Placemakers

in Kilbirnie—we recommend you all go there. We
drove home and built the fence. First we paced out

the placement of the stakes, then we hammered
them in as far as they would go, with me

doing the last bit because my son is not quite
strong enough to deliver a hefty blow. Then we

unwound the black mesh my mother had
given us (she's moving after twenty years.

In the house she and my father built there's
a lot of stuff that needs to go—our accumulated

childhoods, for example. *Mt Egmont from the Southward*,
Papa Small, the fish smoker. A lot of it

has been absorbed into the respective households
of me and my sisters; stuff like the roll of black mesh).

We rolled it out and I stretched and nailed it
onto the posts as my son searched for worms

in the garden. The pallets we laid outside the boys'
shed to make a deck, so they don't stand

on the vegetable garden.
All this cost us $23.50.

*

Just over a year after Nigel died, we drove to Mataikona
to bury his ashes. Three baches on a rough

coast. Children wild as the water. In the evening
we ate together on the walled verandah, candles

lit, coats and scarves against the cold. Next morning
friends and family arrived, then at midday

we called the children from the beach and the bush
and we headed up the steep climb at the back

of the house. Our friend's ashes were passed
from hand to hand on the way up the hill.

Halfway, his mother sat—desolate,
breathless—then resumed the climb.

Nigel's wife and three children buried his ashes under
earth, then named stone. The children planted seeds

of the karaka tree he rested under. Two daffodil bulbs
were placed—one for new growth, one for friendship

so they would never be alone. Next morning, early,
the children headed for the rocks bearing

sticks and buckets, on the hunt for crabs.
Left behind, the smallest of them

hurtled down the paddock, jumped the long, damp grass.
Hey! he cried. *Hey!* All our childhoods

joined with him. In our jackets and gumboots, morning hair;
the oldest ones, the youngest ones, and the ones

in the middle, *Hey!* we cried. Frankie, five—
youngest son of our friend who died—he ran and

climbed the fence, in gumboots, with toast.

*

This poem was always going to end there, with Frankie
and the toast. That image has been the engine

of the poem, but then
more happened.

*

I wanted to write about my father's ashes.
How when we scattered them I was shocked

at how fine and grey and gritted they were.
I was pleased I had read Dave Eggers's book

A Heartbreaking Work of Staggering Genius
in which he describes his astonishment at the feel

of his parents' ashes in his hands. It was from this book
that I knew some of what to expect—see how useful

literature can be. Still, I was amazed.

*

Learn to be slow said a slate work of Denis
O'Connor's. Yes, I am. Illness stopped me

and because I have no desire to revisit
that place, I am wary and stiller than

I ever have been.

*

On my way home from a hospital appointment
I talked to a taxi driver called Bob about *quiet*

and how no one seems to like it any more.
People are always plugged in, listening to something.

I explained that I walk with nothing in my ears but
what's going on, and Bob said *yep* he preferred

the sound of the world because *the sound of the world*
has the sound of reason in it.

*

At the supermarket, on my way to read poems
at a book launch, I remember a letter to the

newspaper from a man who was appalled at the price
of groceries, but said nothing would drive him

to mix with *the type of people who shop*
at PAK'nSAVE. What does he think we'll

do? Bite him?

*

Tomorrow I'm due to get on a plane to fly
to a city to chair a panel of artists talking

about their work. For someone who doesn't like flying
(as one of the characters in *West Wing* says:

'I *experience* flying') or talking in
public, I feel strangely calm about this.

I have agreed to do this thing, both
these things, because since my father

died, and since being ill, I have decided to stop
being afraid.

*

When I was away, I woke early and leaned
out the window into the morning. In the distance

over the city, a hot air balloon ascended.
It was pale. It was perfect. It rose

at just the right speed. It was the ending
to this poem. But then it wasn't.

I closed the window, had breakfast, then a shower,
then gathered my things and went to meet

the others. We packed the car, had coffee
then headed out of town. On the way

we passed a sign which said 'Sing Now'
and so we did.

All time moving

At Barton Marine
I still cannot feel
my heart.

Up ahead,
my mother's old apartment—
fourth floor—pours
water. Towards me comes
a woman, walking,
reading; a thing my son
and husband do. Last year
the son forsook
French art
for books.

My heart remains
unheard from.
Notebook too.
In it there's a recipe
copied
from a waiting-room
magazine.

Chillies, cardamom, bay,
accompany the lamb.
I strike the hill of wool—
here goes the heart,
even at the start
anticipating difficulty.

As at my mother's move—
the speeded beat
as we unpacked boxes
of my father's impossible handwriting
still unable to figure out
what it was
he was saying.

The inner life

I share a bed
with my husband,
an asthma puffer,
and often, under the pillows,
two pens. Life has never been
so good. In the morning
I get up and there are the cups
and saucers—one always to go
with the other.
I feel lucky to know
what a cup of flour
feels like. The way
this flour, with water,
can become bread.
With egg, cake.

Last days

Long days of sun
like the ones
my father died in.
All through the month
the weather held him
the way it held us
through that time—
conversations in chairs
on the terrace outside
his room, eyes shaded
from the glare.
We wondered what came
to him then in those
'solemn moments
of dying'—his parents,
maybe? Our mother?
A shooting trip when he
was younger? Us
in blue corduroy pinafores
plucking geese.

Christmas

Christmas, and I went looking
for presents for the children.

In a toyshop I found myself
standing beside a man I had,
some time ago, spent almost
ten years of my life with.

I said *Hello my old life*—
which is a line
from a Grace Paley story
with one word added.
Hello, he said.

Then we talked about
our mothers and fathers,
sisters and brothers.
He bought Lego and a train set.
Me, a small plastic swimmer
whose arms circled
in a useless hilarious fashion
in water and on land.

Animalia

The telephone rings
and it's raven, calling
from the roof
of the barn.

Outside, there's grass
run through by badgers—
tracks, sett, and signs
of fox.

Our track leads
to a shed
where the piano's skirt
hides a wizened
mouse, window ledge
bed to a dusty bird.
Step outside
and there's a just-dead
vole.

We—the visible, breathing
ones—pick spinach,
sorrel, admire 'Evergreen'
apple; crouch, at night,
in the adamant air.

Tower of London

Be ye cradle salt or blood
Be ye bones or pit of ash
Be ye eye ear or tongue
Be ye tears fire or flood

Be ye rocker stick or crutch
Be ye rip or the knife
Be ye flame smoke or dust
Be ye steady or fucked

Be ye smother or choke
Be ye breath sleep or death
Be ye torpor or fist
Be ye knife gun or rope

Be ye tears fire or flood
Be ye eye ear or tongue
Be ye bones or pit of ash
Be ye cradle salt or blood

Pearly everlasting

Morning strange
and gorgeous. Mist
eiderdowned
into valley, sea a colour
like pearl, like Robert Hass's
'pearly everlasting'.
Two cranes—praying mantises
of the construction world—
transformed by light
into something sculptural
and full of presence. Not
beautiful, exactly, just
not ugly. Winds gale force
forecast for Tuesday.
Lucky for us
the tender anchoring
nouns.

Undone

We watch as all becomes undone.
Your life an unfamiliar house
you live in. Ordinary things sometimes are things of wonder.

Or confusion. Fun done
away with. Others douse
the flames. We watch as all becomes undone.

The seam of every day unpicked to lie among
the others; don't fuss about the mess—
sometimes this too can be a thing of wonder.

The first day of the week's no longer Monday—
all days and weeks are one to those of us
for whom all has become undone.

A watch is of no use to them, nor moon nor sun
for all is one and all is all and they will cast
aside those things that once were things of wonder.

Nothing, now, is clear. All's become con-
fusion. All falls dark. The house closed fast
to light. We watch as everything becomes undone.
Ordinary things that used to be so full of wonder.

Memory

Sometimes we forget that we remember;
find it distressing that the past
could so evade us, remain as merely tremor

in our brains, so that we know the former
life is there, but can't quite grasp
the detail. Sometimes we forget that we remember.

They say to make a house. You can pretend
the rooms are there and in them store fast
memories so they stay whole, more than just a tremor

or a sense of something past. To do this, send
the years upstairs and down. Build shelves to last.
Evict the fact that sometimes we forget that we remember.

One room leads in to another. Extend
the house, add on another room or two, the past
needs storage space, a deck, foundations, so the tremors

of the earth remain as tremors and what is tended
in the house stands fast
and true. Sometimes we forget that we remember.
Feel lucky that the past remains as merely tremor.

Autumn

So careless the trees—
having remembered their leaves
they forget them again
so they fall on us, big
as hands.

Fall and are blown
by the wind
as it talks to the house
and the house
talks back—while inside
babies lick the clocks
until time disappears
inside their gummy mouths.

Fall on my bag, urgent
with talk. On the young man
with hair swirled like water
going down a plughole
and on the plughole
my sister stopped with the gin's
lemon, suggesting later
that a potato
would also do.

Fall on our friends
who have lain down
in the earth
which has remembered that its job
is to take them in so others
can remember them
long after they have joined the dark matter
of its body and the earth itself can forget;

in the way that—because we are human
and used to having arms and legs
and doing things with them—

we forget our own.

Leaves fall on the van
of *Mr Pipe*
the Plumber
on boredom
on the pavement where's chalked
What would you ask him?

Through air bright
with unhappiness,
through thought,
the particular thought
that you are pleased
it's not your job
to remember the names of
all the leaves coming down
because that would be
beyond you—way beyond
you—like the distance, which is a place
you haven't been to, but hope
to visit some day.

Somehow the leaves
make you remember
and remember
and remember some more
and all this remembering
is very tiring, so tiring
that you need to make somebody

a sandwich, a sandwich of leaves,
which luckily there are a lot of,
falling so steadily as they are,
and as it's the end of the day
you can take this sandwich down
to the beach, where, you remember,
there's always sand and sometimes
a wedding.

Full Moon

The moon came up
and all our thinking
went sideways.
I dreamed the children
ate my lunch. The children
who sleep now, worn out
by the effort of coming—
through tears and nature—
to themselves.
I got up to watch the moon
fall on them—make light
of their hair, their stubbornness,
their long accommodating arms.
The wind blew great drifts of sadness
all about—many leaves having gathered
for this effect.
Each leaf, when loosed
from its tree, makes a sound
like the finest grade of sandpaper
engaged in work.
Each time a leaf brushes past
it rubs off a bit of you
rubs a bit of you off.

Poem about a horse

This poem could be about your horse.
This horsc here, or a horse
you remember, either one will be fine

and either way you will need to include
some other animal to keep the horse
company. This could be your friend's dog—

your friend from childhood who spent
a lot of time in trees and climbed down
once, with you not noticing, still reading

in the tree hut. Or your sister's guinea pigs—
again from childhood—eating up the back
lawn. At a stretch, it could be the chocolate reindeer

you bought and carried around in your pocket
all day, though that's not much company
for a horse. Yaks could be good. The yaks

you heard about from the nice young man who sold you
your phone—the global roaming one. His uncle
was a yak farmer who lived next door to an Amish

community. In exchange for wool they helped him
build his house—big, so the yaks could come
inside. Tables and chairs were nailed to the floor

so the animals wouldn't knock them over
as they wandered about the kitchen. Yes,
a yak could be good. Once, when I was global

roaming—high above the earth, trembling
towards home—the lights below were soft
and woolly, just like a yak, I thought. So,

your horse might like a yak for company.
I myself would like that, though a yak
certainly wouldn't fit inside our house,

not the way it is at present. We could always get
a tradesman to widen the doorways and fix
the furniture, but our record with tradesmen is hardly

spectacular. We attract the kind of man who is very nice,
but whose personal circumstances—surfing and a new
fiancée, for instance—mean he starts a job but never

finishes. This accounts for things like the very long skirting board
which sticks up and out from behind our sofa like a piece of wood
you might tie an old pillowcase to to prevent other people

driving into it as you deliver it to the tip. We wouldn't invite
that particular tradesman back to yak-proof the house.
Your horse might prefer a hare or quail. Both appear

at dusk, so you could introduce them then. They also like it
after a thunderstorm, the sort that comes quickly, out of
nowhere, so you're stuck barbecuing rain.

Once you've settled on your animal, your horse might need a drink,
and by then, of course, it could be evening, the time of day when
light flees for safety in the hills. The poem can wait. It's time now

to stable your horse. If it's the horse that's here, that's an easy matter;
but if it's the horse you've remembered, you'll need to also remember
the stable and the colour of the girl's shoes as she took the horse inside

last night to settle. What was on her mind as she led the horse, clip
clop, through the stable door? Was it the boy with the voice like
a river? Or was it the river with a boat that would take her to the house

of the man who, for heaven's sake, was old enough to be
her father? You'll need to think about that. And her shoes? Were they
her sister's or her brother's? The colour of the sky needs to be

remembered, the state of the moon, and which bird made a racket;
and then, most importantly, you'll need to forget that sound,
deep inside your ear, which is the sound of the world unravelling itself.

May

Outside
the cold is startling,
visible.

One tree broadcasts red
among its neighbours—
not lovely, exactly, just
not green. A gecko
in the washing, crumpled
like a glimpse of slate sky
through a cloud
of sheets—perfect
piece of winter.
Despite all night
in the machine, not dead,
just shocked and clean.

And us, our limbs in bed
like those of startled
horses—skittish, mad
for warmth.

And even though
there's no snow
this far north,
I like to think of Rabelais
who wrote in his 'Pantagruel'
of battle sounds trapped
in the ice.
When spring came around
and thaw began
they once again
were heard.

Us,
what would we
preserve?

Time

We woke
to spring nuzzling at
the window.
Winter's passed, like
last night's hail
in the gin.
Frozen puddle
in the freezer
a reminder;
like our son's
placenta, still there
after eleven years—
us frozen
by indecision,
which tree
and where?
Sons grown to men.
One sister blown
away, two
here to stay.
Time passes quickly
in this bed,
the child said.

Forty fifty

It is
quite plainly
spring. Coffee
like a spell—
Medellin Excelso
Colombian.
Children out
on the long driveway
to adulthood, us
at its edge
in search of Rue
'that sour herb
of grace'.
When we were
children here
there used to be
ducks. In the blare
of sunlight
someone says
It feels like
Spring.   *It is,*
we say.
It's here.
It's now.

Index of titles

Index of books